TRAINING FOR THE MARATHON OF LIFE

What happens when we choose Jesus as our life coach?
Simply and logically, Peter Watson Jenkins presents.
the authentic teaching of Jesus of Nazareth
as a training course for a better world.
It is training that we can all follow—if we dare.

Choosing Jesus As Our Life Coach

TRAINING FOR THE MARATHON OF LIFE

Peter Watson Jenkins

Resource *Publications*

An imprint of *Wipf and Stock Publishers*
199 West 8th Avenue • Eugene OR 97401

TRAINING FOR THE MARATHON OF LIFE
By Peter Watson Jenkins, MA.

Copyright © 2005 Peter Watson Jenkins. All rights reserved.
Except for brief quotations in critical publications or reviews, no part of this book may be reproduced in any manner without prior written permission from the publisher. Write: Permissions, Wipf & Stock, 199 W. 8th Ave., Eugene, OR 97401.

ISBN: 1-59752-447-6

Manufactured in the U.S.A.

FIRST EDITION

Dedicated to the Memory of Thomas Jefferson

President of The United States of America

Editor of

The Life and Morals of Jesus of Nazareth

*

"We must reduce our volume to the simple evangelists, select, even from them, the very words of Jesus. There will be found the most sublime and benevolent code of morals which has ever been offered to man."

Thomas Jefferson

Letter to John Adams, 13th October 1813

CONTENTS

	Foreword	ix
Part I: MAKING A PLAN FOR LIFE		1
	Socrates and the Marathon	3
	A Coach for All Seasons	10
	Preparing for the Race	14
	Revising the Training Manual	15
	Outline of the Training Course	20
Part II: THE COACH'S WORDS OF WISDOM		27
The Kingdom:	Jesus' Prayer	29
	What Is the Kingdom?	31
	When will the Kingdom Come?	33
	What will the Kingdom change?	34
Values for Our Life:	The Great Consolation	37
	Our Basic Attitudes	39
	Giving Up Power and Wealth	41
Personal Qualities:	Shrewdness	43
	Persistent Patience	45
	Honesty and Integrity	47
	Openness	49
	Care for Others	52
	Forgiveness	55
A Summary of Jesus' Teaching		61
Part III: TURNING WORDS INTO DEEDS		63
	Dreams and Utopias	63
	Reform Movements	71
	Jesus' Vision for Humanity	77
	Planning for The Good Society	93
	People who Changed Society	101
	Running the Marathon of Life	105
	A Check List for Activists	117
APPENDIX		
	I. Notes on the Text	121
	II. Bibliography	135

FOREWORD

Each of us needs to develop realistic goals for living the best we can. Our plan should give us a sense of purpose as individuals and also contribute to the welfare of human society. To make such a plan we must first find a coach to instruct and encourage us. Jesus of Nazareth is such a coach. Whether we are Christian or not, we will find in his core teaching, stripped of historical additions, a dynamic training course for the personal marathon we must run through life.

Jesus' original practical teaching is presented here in all its dynamic and honest simplicity. I hope every reader will be challenged by his words. The book explores the wealth of his instruction for today's world— a truly revolutionary plan, not only for personal growth but also for the reclamation of society from its polarization and disaster.

My gratitude goes to those who first taught me by their love the way of Jesus of Nazareth, especially my parents, sister, and nanny; and those patient souls who gave me a vision of biblical scholarship, my tutors at Cheshunt College and Cambridge Divinity School, especially Dr. Eric Pyle and Dr. Jack Newport, and student friends Dr. John Hull, Rev. John Berryman, and Rev. Jonathan Creamer, with whom I argued theology over coffee into the wee small hours of the night.

Those who have helped me with the content and presentation of this book are sincerely thanked, including Dr. Perry Kea and Dr. Austin Ritterspach, of the Department of Philosophy and Religion, University of Indianapolis; Dr. Robert Funk, Director of the Westar Institute and Founder of the Jesus Seminar; Angela Gluck Wood, religious writer and broadcaster; members of the British Unitarian Church Publications Committee; my publisher Jim Tedrick of Wipf and Stock; and Sonia Ness, my dear wife and copy editor, without whose loving enthusiasm this book would never have been completed.

Peter Watson Jenkins
Elk Grove Village, Illinois

PART I
MAKING A PLAN FOR LIFE

Most people stop doing things occasionally to reflect about life itself and their purpose in being here. We all need to ask ourselves questions of that sort or everything we do spins out of control. Human beings rush from one activity to another with very little sense of direction, but deep inside, nearly all of us have a personal agenda for the things we do. When we actually get around to thinking about such things, we will discover just how essential and rewarding it can be to actually plan to live a fulfilling and satisfying life. One of the main reasons why people go to houses of worship is to be involved in such an activity.

All of us can find the principles of a plan for successful living. It has to be a plan that holds good from the cradle to the grave: one that we can readily persuade ourselves to follow and—having mastered—teach to the next generation. So our life must come to reflect openly the principles we have chosen, and from which we draw strength.

Brian

Looking around at the world, you can often pick out remarkable people who appear totally in control of their lives. I felt that about my high school friend Brian. When we were seventeen, our class considered Brian the very best guy in town. He was good-looking, smart, hardworking, talented, and above all, nice to be around. His teachers liked him because he was conscientious with his schoolwork. His classmates thought he was a cool sportsman, great with the girls, and someone with whom they could share a laugh. Luckily, I had my desk near his in class and also met him out of school at the youth group in a downtown church. He was just the same there, equally popular with the guys and the girls. He danced well, didn't drink much, took church seriously (but not over-piously), and never, to my knowledge, made his friends feel ill at ease. I met Brian several years after leaving school. He had a lovely wife, a couple of kids, and a great job. He appeared to be just the same, a truly terrific individual.

Brian comes to mind because I think he must have been one of those people with a personal plan for life that really worked. When we were schoolboys we never gave such an idea sustained thought, of course. In fact, I wonder if he had decided on any specific personal agenda at that time, one with the precise details of what he was going to do each day. But he must have had a broad vision of how to tackle whatever challenged him from time to time. Perhaps what he learned at home, school, and church had helped him to be like that.

Take school homework assignments for example. I guess Brian needed some prodding at times—perhaps his parents even had a struggle training him at first—but he certainly learned how to do the dreadful stuff. He learned to understand that neat homework, well finished and checked for mistakes, and handed back in a well-cared-for exercise book wins teachers' approval every time. When you are the captain of the rugby team, coming top in class is cool.

Unlike my idol, I was one of those boys who spent the evening at home trying to do as little homework as possible, drawing pictures of imaginary houses or reading novels, and frequently leaving my school task to the very last minute. Often, when I was tired and ready for bed, the homework still had to be done. Only then did a mixture of fear and conscience motivate me to get down to my books.

Life starts with simple demands—having sharp pencils, neat exercise books, and good homework—but as we get older it becomes more complicated. Our attitude toward how we set about solving small problems reaches into every aspect of our life. We learn how to face up to our little difficulties and make a personal plan to overcome them, a process that prepares us to overcome the future's inevitably larger problems and challenges.

Character

Eventually, the character we develop shows the results of our struggles with personal challenges of all kinds. Do we grumble, because grumbling is part of our inner plan? Are we dishonest about little things and even big things on occasion? Do we tell lies to other people, just as we lied to our teacher about the dog eating our workbook? Or are the standards we maintain those of integrity and endurance, that we don't let slip, even when we're under pressure.

Any well-thought-out plan for life involves knowing how to organize our time and effort. Time management is a very practical thing. Some companies give their managers books in which to write down their personal goals for each day. All over the world, thousands of motivational speakers are paid handsome fees to lecture us on setting goals and managing priorities.

I remember a dear friend telling me about one of those sessions. Her group had been taught that when they pick up a piece of paper from their desk at work—a memo, a letter, or an invoice—they should do everything possible to finish that task before going on to the next one. Completing assignments that way demonstrates a good work agenda.

Some people try to run their whole life in that manner, setting daily goals and tackling one job at a time. I had a manager once who lived that way but he seemed far too programmed for my liking. He made his program something he worshiped! Of course, an agenda for life must cover many more activities than a business plan. It's hard to be well organized, even at work. Living in a mess is easy, and it can be more comfortable for our ego. "Look at this pile of work I have to get through!" we say to our co-workers as we shuffle our papers. But deep down we envy anyone who has a neat desk and nearly all tasks completed by the end of each day.

Socrates and the Marathon

My personal search for the right lifetime agenda began with a jump-start when I was a freshman college student in England. One wet November in 1954, I was in bed for about ten days suffering from glandular fever, which was especially painful in my throat. It was an unwelcome pause in the carefree life of a work-shy undergraduate, but it provided an opportunity to do a little of that essential personal thinking I noted earlier. The radio in the bedroom had died of a broken heart, and my family did not own a television, so there wasn't much else to do but think or read. It's surprisingly easy to remember clearly what took place, even though it all happened over fifty years ago.

At the time, I did not consider myself desperately unhappy about anything in my life. Mixing in a large circle of student friends was fun. We all found studies interesting, even if they were quite difficult at times. It was true that my parents seemed to have a different plan for my future from my own, but success seemed to lie on the road ahead and I was reasonably content—except for the problem of religion.

You really get to know what the practice of religion is like when you grow up in a Christian minister's home. My father, a truly self-disciplined man, was theologically a moderately liberal Methodist minister. Our family was not overwhelmingly devout, but the Christian faith was taken very seriously. As a result, my older sister and I went to church quite happily as children, although our parents did not allow us to attend Sunday school for reasons that were never fully explained to me. I think they believed that parents were the natural teachers of the family faith, and they did not need any help. So, while I was very small, my dear Nanny took me for walks during the sermon. After she had left us to become a nurse during the Second World War, I was made to sit quietly beside my mother, who gripped my hand tightly whenever I wriggled too much. I always sit rather still in church these days.

We often talked religion at the dinner table on Sunday. I remember my sister, an accomplished intellectual from an early age, discussing modern biblical textual scholarship with father for so long on one occasion that even mother got bored and brought the meal to a welcome end. I did not know it then, but the scholarly terms they used that day, when talking about different types of biblical analysis, would become familiar to me when I was in training for the Christian ministry at Cambridge University several years later.

Revolt

Like many young adults, I became restless with the pattern of life in the home, and restless at being part of a professing Christian family, but the fun of belonging to the large youth group at church long delayed my youthful rejection of the Christian religion. In the end, however, I told myself it was no longer possible to accept the ancient doctrines of the faith, because their truth could not be truly verified. Despite my father's joyful proclamation, I no longer believed that Jesus rose from the dead on the third day; and he was not "the only begotten Son of God, co-equal and co-eternal with the Father and the Holy Spirit in the unity of the Godhead." I wondered who needed to believe in God, and wrote mean-spirited and trite doggerel about my friendly and supportive church, which began, "I remember, I remember, the place where I was bored." It wasn't really true, but it felt good to "come out" as an agnostic to my student friends, with whom, interestingly, I never stopped talking about religion. Now I was free at last to think my own thoughts and plan my own destiny. There was nothing unusual in this youthful personal re-positioning; it happens all the time. I was just a fairly typical young person seeking independence.

Then, lying on my sick bed, thinking about life, I wondered what was the point of it all. If the existence of God couldn't be proved, and if Jesus was merely a religious teacher who lived a long time ago, what followed? Wasn't the only possible judgment on my family's religious activity that it was largely a waste of time? If there wasn't a God to live for, we didn't have to live according to His rules. I got that far in my thinking with a measure of certainty, but what followed after this spirited denial of my family's religious basis was not at all easy to work out.

An Examined Life

What finally got me thinking was this question: If people don't believe in God, by what principles should they try to live? Was it enough simply to obey and uphold those civil and criminal laws that my friends and I were busy studying? The caustic comments about traditional religion that our rationalist professor of jurisprudence made in class were never far from my mind. I was convinced we all had to have rules to live by, clear ethical rules. Where people have given scant observance of law and morality, societies have fallen apart rapidly. But the rule of law was not enough, even for this law student. We all had to have something more satisfying, something that could be written in our hearts.

As my fever began to subside, I felt able at last to do some reading. The dusty books on the bedroom shelf seemed only vaguely interesting; nevertheless one finally caught my eye. It was a small blue book, printed in 1891, with a dated translation of the Greek philosopher Plato's *Trial and Death of Socrates*. I still have the book today; it is a treasured companion. On the opening page was a Greek quotation from Plato, translated by F. J. Church: "An unexamined life is not worth living."

The idea caught my fancy and I hastened to begin reading. In the book, Plato recounted stories of the life and teaching of his mentor, Socrates. The volume ended with the great teacher taking the poison hemlock after he had been condemned to death by the Athenian authorities. There was much more to Plato's account of the teaching of Socrates than the short passage that captured my youthful attention that day, but what I read made so much sense that it changed my life! It's odd how these things happen. Something you read with true amazement may mean little or nothing to somebody else who will be left quite unmoved. Yet you receive the idea joyfully as a revelation, altering the very way you think and act from that time on. That's what happened to me that day. In the life-changing passage I read, Socrates was telling Crito how we learn the right way to live:

> *Socrates:* *Should we think highly of everyone's opinions or just those of a handful of people? Should we rate highly sound judgments and reject worthless ones?*

(Crito, whom Plato never allowed to talk for long in reply, agreed that we should take notice of the sound judgments that good people make.)

> *Socrates:* *Does someone who is in training for the marathon race, and is serious about it, listen to the advice of everybody, or to the one man who is his coach?*
>
> *Crito:* *He listens to the advice of the one man.*
>
> *Socrates:* *Then he must exercise, and eat, and drink, in whatever way his coach, who understands the matter, tells him and not as others advise?*
>
> *Crito:* *That's right.*
>
> *Socrates:* *And if he disobeys his coach, and disregards his opinion, and takes notice instead of the many people who understand nothing about training, will he not suffer in consequence? And where will he suffer?*
>
> *Crito:* *His body will suffer, for sure.*
>
> *Socrates:* *You're right. But isn't this the same in everything? In questions of right and wrong, of what is honorable and what is base, of good and evil, ought we to follow the many, or*

accept the opinion of the one man who understands these matters?

I knew the answer to that one. Of course I should follow the one teacher who truly understands life. So I read on and on with eager anticipation, hoping that Socrates would turn out in the end to be that suitable trainer or coach for me, which was Plato's opinion, of course.

Socrates' idea appealed strongly because of its downright practicality. As an amateur rugby player (though definitely not a long-distance runner), I could identify with the marathon runner-in-training. As an insecure college student, I could recognize my need for sound guidance from a skilled and successful mentor. In less than a page, Socrates' argument had succeeded in pointing me in a new direction: to take a fresh look at Jesus' teaching as a "Christian outsider."

Student life might have been comfortable, but I was not truly happy. I enjoyed some success, especially in student politics and in debates at the Student Union, but I knew my success was largely a matter of technique and not of substance. Reading this book by Plato convinced me that I was setting out on the race of life without a trainer to whom I could relate. Suddenly that seemed like a bad mistake.

Trainers

For a while, Socrates headed a short list of possible trainers. People in church had told me that Dr. Albert Schweitzer had led a highly successful life, but I did not know enough about his story to understand why they got so excited about his "leaving everything behind" and leaving Europe to work in the African jungle at Lambaréné. At that time, nobody had explained Schweitzer's doctrine of "Reverence for Life," and I did not bother to find out. Nobody had introduced me to the Mahatma Gandhi's non-violent doctrine of "Truth Force" either, so he was ignored along with many others. As I have said before, I did not relate well to homework.

Among the great religious teachers of the past, the Buddha, Confucius, Lao-Tze, and the Prophet Mohammed were non-starters, because of my prejudice and ignorance. My aging contemporary Winston Churchill was given a passing thought, but I knew that he was a great wartime leader rather than a teacher of a lifestyle. There wasn't even one woman up for consideration on my list; it took me three decades to realize that mistake. These days, I have a wider choice, but in the damp days of November 1954 there was only one contender that I could identify to be my coach for the Marathon of Life.

It was more than a little scary to think that I should interview Jesus of Nazareth for the training job. Not wanting to believe most of the things that other people said about Jesus, and seeking to continue my broad rejection of the Church's doctrines, made it really hard to accept that he could even be a candidate at all. I also had a gut feeling, formed by listening to numerous sermons, that Jesus might interview me, not the other way round.

In the end I made a decision on the basis of what my gut told me, that Jesus of Nazareth, unique or not, should be offered the job of personal guide, philosopher, and friend. Obviously he was a great teacher, whose words had stood the test of time. Other people had found his teaching helpful in their lives. I didn't think anyone still thought quite as highly of Socrates. In my overwhelmingly Christian community, public acceptance of Jesus made a great impression on me. In the fifties there was more churchgoing in Britain than in these days. I had even attended a local Billy Graham revival on a telephone link from the London stadium, but it left me cold.

Jesus of Nazareth

Then the idea dawned that there were two ways to look at Jesus of Nazareth. Both were important in my childhood, but now they could be viewed separately. The first was as *the Christ of Faith*; that divine person whom my father proclaimed as the resurrected Lord, and through whom he addressed simple and eloquent prayers to God in the Methodist chapels I attended when he was preacher there for the day.

But there was another Jesus, *the Jesus of History*, about whom the stories of my childhood had been lovingly told. Now I recognized that I might dig down into the facts about Jesus and throw out all the bits other people had added, bits I knew existed from our family's dinner table conversations. Then I might just be able to find out what my new coach had actually said all those years ago. So, if I listened to him alone and put aside the interpretations others had made, maybe it would be possible to find the right way to run the marathon of life, which stretched bewilderingly ahead of me.

Despite that cautious start, within six months of making my choice I had softened my attitude to Christianity, submitting in genuine humility to many of the doctrines of the Church, hoping them to be correct. It was a state of obedience to the Jesus of Protestant Christianity which lasted for about twenty years. Eight years after reading Socrates, I was ordained as a Congregational minister and worked in and out of the parish scene. Then, following a church merger, refusing to accept my church's beefed-up doctrinal requirements for both its ministers and its people, I quit the new (British) United Reformed Church to join the Unitarians, a more liberal church tradition, and finally dropped out of parish ministry altogether.

Now the wheel has turned full circle and I have come back to think that Jesus' core teaching, as described in this book, still provides a powerful direction for my life, although now I have insights from a host of teachers, both women and men, whose honestly successful lives have taken me to new depths of understanding. The church's dogma about Jesus of Nazareth continues to fog my simple view of his life as a man who really made no claim to be God, and who lived as a religious teacher (possibly aspiring to be the Jewish Messiah) in a world that was both skeptical and superstitious at the same time. I suspect that many who call themselves Christian today have similar difficulties over the niceties of belief, which they carefully hide from the faithful around them in the church for fear of being criticized or shunned.

Looking back now, it is clear to me that the choice of Jesus of Nazareth was probably the only one I was capable of making at the time. What I did not realize was that my attitude toward the story and record of Jesus' teaching, which I thought so radical, was fundamentally a mainstream liberal approach to the Bible and the Christian faith. That liberalism has never left me, and, to the bewilderment of family and friends, it provides me with the basis on which I can honestly accept the teaching of Jesus today.

In this book, I want to put my own views aside and to present Jesus' core teaching simply and plainly. It is immensely important to me to reveal the content of my coach's teaching in its original form. After that, you may draw conclusions about what you believe and whatever plan of action for life may evolve for you.

A Coach for All Seasons

After making my choice, and still on my sickbed, I put Plato aside and devoured the New Testament gospels, writing out bits of what Jesus had said into a little dog-eared Edwardian notebook my mother had given me. It was a primitive attempt, but there's nothing quite so rewarding as doing something like that for oneself. It left an indelible mark on my mind.

This happened in England where few people know that, 150 years before, with greater scholarship and sophistication, Thomas Jefferson, the third President of the United States of America, had attempted much the same search. In 1804 he found time from public duties to make his famous scissors-and-paste selection from the gospels, which he called *The Life and Morals of Jesus*, but which is better known today as *The Jefferson Bible* (Appendix II). A theological layman who was well ahead of his time, Jefferson sensed what biblical scholars have worked hard over subsequent generations to evaluate: that we have lost contact with the original thrust of the teaching of Jesus.

A true picture of the Teacher himself is hard to find in the mass of personal opinions, fables, and ideas that have been added to his life story and to his original words. It is also true that Jesus repeated some of the wisdom of his day, a practice some Christians may find hard to acknowledge, preferring to believe that everything he said must have been unique. Rather, his uniqueness lay in *how* he taught and *what* he selected to talk about.

Change was now the order of the day for me, and the practical results of appointing Jesus of Nazareth as my coach were dramatic. Before long, dripping with excitement at his words that I discovered in the gospels, I had changed many things in my life, spurred on by a simple and rather literal understanding of his teaching.

Soon I embraced pacifism and precipitously dropped out as the leader of the student Conservative Party, where there had been very real possibilities of my developing a serious political career. Because of Jesus' teaching about non-violence, I registered two years later for alternative National Service as a conscientious objector, serving my country first as a forestry worker in Scotland and, later, as an orderly in a London hospital, rather than being drafted into the military. Nine years later, I worked as the executive director of a British pacifist organization, the Fellowship of Reconciliation.

Inconsistency

It is sadly necessary to record that for long stretches of time since 1954, my coach has not received from me the understanding or acceptance his teaching deserves. During these periods, as Socrates might say, I have preferred to stop in the marketplace and listen to the conflicting advice from the guys sitting at the little café tables. As with my old struggles over homework, so with marathon running: I have been neither consistent nor conscientious as a student, and my performance has varied a good deal in consequence. Over the next forty years, I managed to bungle a number of important things and to hurt a good number of people. I'm sorry for all that, especially for friends and loved ones who have suffered from an overdose of my selfishness.

Nevertheless, today I'm more certain than ever that we live life in the best way when we have a good coach to follow. I know in my heart now, as never before, that it isn't too late to listen to the advice of the trainer I selected all those years ago.

It's one thing to find a coach and quite another to retain our confidence in the training we have received. If my enthusiasm for the teaching of Jesus of Nazareth has been inconsistent, one reason is that the Christian church has turned him into a mystical, magical figure, divorced from everyday life. Periodically, I have fallen for this unbelievable picture of him, and have retreated from wanting to grapple with his down-to-earth message. It may have been selfishness in part, but also a direct consequence of the super-human image of Christ presented by the church.

The second reason for my inconsistency in following his teaching was the practical problem of finding out what Jesus of Nazareth had actually said, and of truly understanding what he meant. Perceiving this difficulty has led to the writing of this book. It's hard to talk about the teacher from Galilee in a non-traditional way when most people seem to be deeply offended that you should even *think* of doing so. It's hard to assemble the fragments of his teaching in an order that speaks meaningfully to our present difficult human world situation. Teaching has to be presented in the right way to train the mind. The four gospels' jumbled and somewhat contradictory records simply do not do the job well enough; if they had, we would not possess so many books attempting to clarify things for us.

Views about Jesus

For most Christians, Jesus is the Lord and Savior of the world. It feels wonderful to call him that if you are already a believer, but this claim makes it hard for people outside the church to seriously consider his teaching. In addition, in most of its denominations, the Church doesn't stop at a simple account of his life and teaching, but expects us to believe the stories about a divine Jesus, his virgin birth, his miracles, his visitation of hell, his resurrection, and his ascension into heaven. That's a tough demand for a generation trained to verify statements. Many regular people don't want to make a commitment to any leader without first having all their questions answered with unassailable facts.

We need to build a bridge of understanding between those holding traditional attitudes of the Christian faith and other, equally sincere, inquirers after truth. To be acceptable, any trainer must be understandable. Fortunately, so far as I have viewed him, the real Jesus of Nazareth was that sort of man. Whether or not he was the promised Messiah does not affect my life in any real way. In his reported healing of other people, if it took place, he most likely used well-authenticated techniques that thousands of spiritual and psychic healers have employed for centuries, and that are still in use today.

Most of Jesus' teaching was an amalgam of other people's ideas and stories with an individual, refreshing twist to them. The account of his death on a cross, which is hailed by Christianity as the ultimate act of self-giving by the God of Love to reconcile the sinful human race to its Divine Creator, is what people have said about him, not what he said about himself. There are inadequate and conflicting explanations in the gospels for Jesus' death, and a serious lack of contemporary records about the event. Certainly for me, as for many modern biblical scholars, the detailed stories of his rising from the dead were a later addition made by his supporters.

Clearly, Jesus of Nazareth was a clever, forthright, and courageous man. Scholars have noted that he called himself *Son of Man*. This was a current Jewish term meaning "a human being." Despite some biblical interpretations of the phrase being used in a heroic way, it was a title his followers quickly dropped from major use after his death. I think some of them wanted to have a hero who was twice life-size or more, and they certainly set about trying to prove it.

In today's critical world, however, rather than wanting a superman, many people need a life-size Jesus who can be clearly seen to have lived a recognizably human life and to have died an understandable human death. The fact that he came up with challenging ideas about how to tackle the business of facing the rough and tumble of everyday existence should be enough for us. We all know that his wave of ideas sparked an enormous social revolution. It is a wave still racing toward the shore of human society with considerable force, despite the uncertainty surrounding his words and the question of who he might have been.

That's how I see my coach. I've followed him now for over fifty years and don't see reason to change. I'm disappointed how little of his advice I have taken. Perhaps, instead of losing that little Edwardian notebook my mother gave me, I should have worked on his sayings rather longer to get the details of his teaching right first time.

Please don't be disappointed if I don't believe in Jesus exactly as you do. There's plenty of room in the world for us all to think different thoughts. I'm happy to have selected Jesus to be my coach. In the end, each one of us has to work out our inner way of understanding the issues of religion. So we finish up with having many kinds of Christians. The old joke of each little group of the faithful needing to go to a separate walled garden in heaven, so they can be with folks they like, is right in one respect. God seeks all of us. He blesses our poor, myopic faith richly and without ceasing. The one thing we must never, ever do is to set out to distort the faith in order to control other people. That's been tried and always fails in the end. It's time we listened to the voices of the serious biblical students who have done their homework and are now able to present us all with the very clear message the great teacher left for us to consider and to live by.

Preparing for the Race

Now let's get down to the job of preparing to run the marathon of life. Although running isn't my scene, and may not be yours, the marathon metaphor has been valuable. After all, have we not all seen television pictures of thousands of runners starting one of those races, and watched the best of them happily breasting the tape at the finish line?

The course for our marathon of life is numbered in years from our birth. The end of the race, death, is usually around the corner, out of sight. Unlike those taking part in an Olympic marathon, we all travel at the same speed—one second at a time—so this race calls to mind the famous Olympic Games declaration that success for athletes should not be measured by their winning but by their taking part. We run this race in a way familiar to all the best athletes. What counts the most is knowing that we have tried consistently hard and have sometimes beaten our previous personal best. Holding such an attitude may attract the attention of others, but the most important thing is the satisfaction we can feel in our personal achievement as the marathon of life goes along.

As we near the finish line, we hope to reflect on how well we have done. By the end of life we should have learned some lessons and gained a grain of wisdom, not mere book learning but the sort one gets through real, tough living. It should not matter to us whether we have been materially successful, providing we have been adept in maintaining good relationships with friends and loved ones and with a host of more distant people. One important mark of our success in living will be the record of the things we did for others and for society as a whole.

There are blind alleys and dead ends we can run down. One is the pursuit of pleasure for its own sake, without thought for other people's comfort and safety. Another may be the conquest of weaker people in our relentless quest for power—not just political power, but also material or sexual power; the sort of maltreatment that leaves other people bruised, gasping for breath, and scarred for life.

Some things we will have achieved are less important than others. Personal comfort in old age is generally agreed by our generation to be a worthy goal. Not everyone can make their retirement comfortable; sometimes personal sacrifices to help others along the way have been too important. Perhaps they were consumed by the great campaigns to bring peace to the world, to save endangered species and the environment, to rescue the poor and suffering, to build up society, or to triumph over personal difficulties of the mind and body.

Some of us may have not done any of these laudable things very much, except in giving fairly trivial support to projects promoting social change for the better. Perhaps our family has taken first place in our life; perhaps the task of living with a difficult spouse or aged parent has consumed all our strength; perhaps grinding poverty or physical or mental disability was an inescapable fact of a difficult life. Achieving material success means nothing worthwhile if greed and self-centeredness have impoverished our personality.

Unlike other kinds of races, in the marathon of life we do not have to achieve only one specific goal. There are many goals, just as there are many starting points for life itself. The marathon of life is essentially an inner personal test of our integrity and moral achievement; it is much less a test of our acceptability in the eyes of our human companions. In the long run, this is why a coach's words of wisdom can be so important to us. They are the best measure by which we can go on judging ourselves, and a useful measure by which our society can be judged, as well.

Revising the Training Manual

Let me explain how Jesus of Nazareth's teaching has been selected for this book. Some readers may know something about this process, but most are unaware of the long, slow development of thinking among biblical scholars to which I shall refer. It is vital that we discover Jesus' authentic words if we are to fully become his students. The lack of true connection with the "real" Jesus is a problem that has made many good people shy of choosing him as their coach in the past.

The good news is that, through years of painstaking research, the world's biblical scholars have overcome major uncertainties about the reliability of ancient texts and of their meanings. Today we have a reasonable hope of knowing which ideas Jesus actually expressed while he was alive two thousand years ago, and which ideas have been added by other people to his record.

In this book I will use a selection of Jesus' authentic words identified by a leading group of scholars. It's a very much smaller number of sayings than the familiar gospels contain, because, the scholars assert, in their effort to remember Jesus' ministry decades later, the evangelists added many comments, and even sayings, to explain what they felt about him.

Let us start by going back again to 1804, when President Jefferson took scissors and paste and made a selection from the gospels, cutting out passages he thought were superfluous in order to concentrate on Jesus' original words and life story. At that time there were few people bold enough to challenge the Bible record in that sort of way, although a few years before, in 1776, the German scholar Johann Griesbach had begun that literary task when he published a synopsis of the first three gospels. Thomas Jefferson believed the three gospel writers Matthew, Mark, and Luke had added their own thoughts and opinions to the simple story about Jesus, and that John's gospel was clearly full of his own ideas interpreting Jesus' life and work, and not at all close to his teacher's original words.

President Jefferson was known to be a religious radical, but he was never in the mainstream of biblical scholarship. He actually kept rather quiet about his bold experiment, except in letters to close friends. But soon after him, clever students of the Bible, including three German scholars, Carl Lachman (1835), Christian Weisse (1838), and Christian Wilke (1838), began to look critically at the gospel records. Slowly a new picture began to emerge about the books of the New Testament.

People already knew that the Church took several generations before coming to an agreement on which books to keep and which to leave out of the New Testament. One of the books left out, for example, was a very early book, claiming to be of Jesus' sayings, called *The Gospel of Thomas*. On the other hand, a very much later book, *The Revelation of St. John*, containing obscure apocalyptic writings, was retained in the New Testament by the Church.

As newly discovered ancient manuscripts of the Bible started to trickle in from old monastic libraries and archeological sites, scholars noted an important aspect of the written record. There was no such thing as a single text of the Bible, as had been previously assumed. Each new manuscript had variations of its own. Mostly they were small in nature, but sometimes they posed major questions concerning its content or the intention of the author. As a result, the scholars began to move away from the simple belief that just one text or one translation could be said to represent "The Word of God," as the Bible had been declared in the past and is still regarded by many Christians.

As the biblical work went on, the loose-knit but growing international body of scholars began to concentrate on the same issues Jefferson had in mind: Who was Jesus of Nazareth? What did he actually say and do? There were important differences within the Bible itself on these points, and it was becoming clear that the publication of the New Testament gospels had been completed generations after the death of Jesus. That raised doubts as to their reliability, and for a time some scholars began to believe it was even possible that Jesus had never lived at all, but had been the invention of the early Christian church's leaders. This gloomy notion was substantially disproved by evidence from ancient sources outside the Christian community, and was proved to be an over-reaction to the difficulties of working with so many differing biblical texts.

Time passed, the bleak point of view faded, and the scholars pressed on with their research. By the turn of the twentieth century, the painstaking detective work of biblical scholarship, aided by the continuing trickle of newly discovered manuscripts, began to affect the scholars' initial point of view. It was now possible to estimate how the first three gospels had come to be written. Then scholars began work on John's gospel, which was truly very different, being much more literary and imaginative than the others, as Jefferson had observed.

Of the four canonical gospels, Mark's was published first, and both Matthew and Luke used it in their own versions of the story of Jesus. Most biblical scholars believe that these two writers also used their own material, along with another written source of sixty-two sayings, which we call *Q* for the German word *Quelle*, or *Source*. (See a note about *The Lost Gospel* in Appendix II.) At the time when the evangelists wrote, the young church was experiencing persecution as well as growing pains, so all the writers added their own ideas to help their readers grapple with their current difficulties. Each writer belonged to a different Christian group and created his own distinctive interpretation of the words and deeds of Jesus, sometimes conflicting with other accounts. Each had a contemporary twist, normal in such writing in those days. Luke, for example, was a well-educated Greek writer with particularly strong views about the nature and origin of Jesus. He was alone among the gospel writers in recounting a story about Jesus' virgin birth.

The lost Gospel of Thomas, known about for a long time, is an archeological discovery of the last century. In 1945 a farmer digging his land near the river Nile discovered a skeleton and a jar containing over a thousand pages of Gnostic writings. This discovery of work by an early religious group triggered substantial archeological activity among tombs in the area. The Gospel of Thomas was one manuscript discovered there.

This Gospel is a collection of over a hundred sayings attributed by the author to Jesus. It has been dated by some scholars as having been written in its original form some time before the other gospels, and is thus an important early witness to the words of Jesus. It suffers like the other gospels, however, from its author having a strong personal agenda, and so it contains many sayings attributed to Jesus that are most unlikely to have been his actual words. Other sayings do closely parallel those found in the first three gospels, with an overlap of about forty sayings with those believed to have come from Q. Scholars have considered that some are in a more original form than those in the four gospels themselves.

Continuing biblical scholarship has produced many new ideas about the scriptures over the years, thereby provoking a great deal of anger from Christians unwilling to modify their belief that the Bible is the "unalterable Word of God." This hostility caused the scholars themselves many years of doubt and difficulty concerning the true meaning of their discoveries. Eventually, however, the scholars became convinced by the evidence before them that, whatever else he might have been, Jesus truly was an historical person with a dynamic message for other people.

So it has taken over two centuries of patient detective work, since

Johann Griesbach's 1776 *Synopsis*, to select Jesus' actual words and phrases from the various accounts written about him years after his death. What some liberal scholars now have agreed may be Jesus' authentic words are only a small part of all the sayings attributed to him in the four gospels themselves. The discussion is far from over, and although there may never be unanimity among liberal scholars, there is a growing agreement as to which biblical texts can be accepted as accurately recording what Jesus said two thousand years ago.

Making Choices

In this book I draw from those stories and teachings that a large team of biblical scholars called The Jesus Seminar have recently stated are probably "the authentic words of Jesus" (Appendix II). These are the precious jewels that one can reasonably believe to be at the core of his teaching, that present a clear account of his philosophy of life.

Sadly, I find many sayings that are old favorites of mine have been left out of the list of those words of whose origin this group of scholars is most certain. This book contains all the passages in the Jesus Seminar's first category: "Jesus undoubtedly said this or something very like it." Some of the most applicable verses in the Seminar's second category, "Jesus probably said something like this," and just a very few others, have also been used in this book.

In new translations of the original Greek, some sayings have verbal changes that make them sound quite different from the old King James Bible text I was first taught in school and church. This gives me sympathy for those who see alterations in the way "modern" people look at Jesus as difficult or next to impossible to accept. But our understanding of the old languages has advanced greatly and we know now that the earliest translations did not always get the meaning right. Better to know what Jesus did say than go on clinging to inaccurate translations of his words just because they sound good.

So, after generations of patient toil, the moment has finally arrived when non-specialist readers can benefit from the complex work that has taken the biblical scholars so long. Much time has been spent unearthing the sacred manuscripts, reading them in the ancient languages, comparing and contrasting them, and puzzling out the reasons for the myriad differences between them. While the search may never be wholly complete, a point has been reached where most of the authentic words of Jesus of Nazareth can be identified, carefully screened by many sincere and dedicated scholars.

Of course, Jesus did not deal with everything that is happening now in the twenty-first century. His overall purpose was to show how people should tackle the job of living. He showed his disagreement with many of the cultural norms of his day concerning family, wealth, honor, and the religious law. He taught the right way was to change the condition of our "heart," so that the law of love written there could be understood.

Most of us go along with society most of the time. We follow the ideas parents and teachers gave us when we were young, and we follow our genetic impulses far more than we know. But there are also less-traveled roads Jesus pointed out, narrower pathways of principle and of unselfishness. He will keep us on the right track for the marathon. It is the race starting with the promise of our birth and, we should hope, ending with our triumph in a life well lived and thoroughly enjoyed.

Outline of the Training Course

Running the marathon of life implies running toward a goal. Jesus sets the goal of life very clearly. We are to fulfill the intention God has for us by becoming citizens of the Kingdom that the divine will has established on earth. This Kingdom is not a heavenly state to be enjoyed after death, but an actual state of living together, here and now. He believed that all people are potential candidates for citizenship of the Kingdom, however good or bad they have been. As an understanding parent, whose forgiveness and loving-kindness are without limit, God allows good and bad people to grow up together, working through the loving actions of those who do understand what life is about, so that even the worst people will eventually be accepted into the renewed society of the Kingdom.

Just as God created an ideal society on earth to which we may belong, so Jesus saw that our entry into it depended upon our relationship with God. He acknowledged God as his intimate father, one who is always willing to give us all our "daily bread," to help us mend broken relationships with others we have hurt or who have hurt us, and to help us overcome our guilt over personal wrongdoing. This gift of divine support, claimed Jesus, is made freely available to us every day, and therefore each day holds out a new opportunity for us to work for the realization of God's Kingdom on earth.

No teacher would be doing a good job if those in training were not enthused with the idea of the final goal. Jesus painted a picture of God's harmonious and attainable society. God's design for humanity is plain. We shall uphold those things sacred to us, and work to create an equitable world where bad deeds are erased, human misery is put to an end, and the worth and dignity of every person is upheld. This human task also achieves the purpose God has for us both as individuals and as a part of humankind. The naturalized citizens of the Kingdom are like children, innocent in their intentions, not double-dealers. They belong to the group in a spirit of humility, trusting the judgment of God for their lives. In leading them into this new order, God helps them to find a personal satisfaction, which often in the past they had felt to be missing.

The new society of the Kingdom comes about because of the common activity of many individuals, including Jesus and his disciples. Above all, his affirmation is that the kingdom is God's work; that God has already established its foundations and created its growth; and that it is God who inspires, enables, and fortifies us to work for its completion. Even weak people with checkered pasts are enabled to contribute to the Kingdom's growth. Eventually, the quality of those involved will speak to all human inadequacy. Then even people who have not foreseen how it is possible for society to change for the better will be able to draw strength from the growing achievements of the Kingdom.

When his disciples responded by asking when and where the Kingdom would make its appearance, Jesus said that it was already in existence but could not be identified easily. He believed that some groups of people had already achieved the goals of the Kingdom. But their work, like a light shining brightly, should have been more readily displayed to encourage other people.

This quest for a new basis of society is not a matter of social organization, let alone political activity. It is something that is first done secretly by God working through individuals. In the middle of a mixed society of good and bad people, the seeds of goodness really are growing. Indeed, when people are successful in achieving their goals, they are often astonished by the impact of the Kingdom in their lives and in the life of their community.

Citizenship

Having explained the goal of the training, Jesus turned to those ..personal qualities people need to achieve that goal. At first sight some of the qualities do not make immediate sense: "Be happy, you poor...you hungry...you who are crying." Jesus saw, as have other religious teachers, that society will never be reformed and people's lives changed unless we turn away from our selfish quest for wealth and share freely with those in need. Just as God sees minutely what is going on in the natural world, so divine care is available to support each individual, however poor, hungry, or helpless they may be. It is a care that is given through other people's practical response to the will of God.

Turning away from the search for personal wealth becomes almost a measuring stick for our beginning as citizens of the Kingdom, as if we have a need to let go of all the props life provides, and apprehend the divine support present in every life at all times. So, Jesus asserted, if we try to preserve our lives, our concentration on self will cause us to lose our vision of what life is all about. Only those who are ready and willing to sacrifice everything for the sake of their vision will discover the full meaning and purpose of existence.

There follows the extension of this paradox. Not only must those wanting to take a lead in establishing a renewed social order be prepared to be servants in society, but also they must accept a rigorous discipline of their minds. They must even be prepared to leave loved ones behind rather than betray the new purpose they have set themselves. They must give all for the sake of the future, and dare all to ensure that the promises of the Kingdom are fulfilled.

Jesus may not have totally condemned wealth, but he clearly saw that the love of possessions of every kind gets badly in the way of the goal we have to set ourselves to be citizens of the Kingdom. Those with wealth must learn to give to those in need, without any show at all, and without requiring repayment of any kind. They must realize that the goal of the perfect society demands an equality of purpose, which is essentially destroyed by some being wealthy and others poor. He pointed to the truly dead-end monomania of those who place the importance of acquisition and retention of wealth as coming before the goal of living an open and meaningful life in relationship with other people.

Despite his discomfort with material possessions, Jesus did not expect people to be without savvy. We need to play our part in society, paying our way, settling our disputes the best we can, escaping from difficult situations with the use of our survival instincts, even paying our dues to the present society while working for its replacement.

One thing is certain: our lives will be judged by their quality, by the standards we maintain, by the purity of our words and thoughts, and by the kindness we show other people and how we think about them. This modesty and integrity lead us to new strategies. Jesus' catch-phrase "Ask, Seek, Knock," suggests fearlessness and downright persistence on the part of those who are dedicated to the task of breaking down the barriers of society and bringing in a renewed way of living under God. It also points to their desire to refer their daily needs to God for divine help.

Just as we need to be kind in our attitudes toward other people, we should be sincere in welcoming them into our lives even though they may be men and women in whose company we would not readily choose to spend time. This new way of life involves a costly process; it is not at all easy to be thoroughly generous to others. We may need to give way so that other people can have a fair share. We must work hard to rescue others who have been treated badly, and it is even likely that some people will not understand or accept our generosity and may try to take advantage of us.

The most generous thing we can do may prove the hardest of all. It is humanly possible to be so little attached to wealth that we have no difficulty parting with it. Yet we have great difficulty in turning with generosity and forgiveness toward those whom we genuinely dislike, or who have hurt us badly, or who consider themselves to be our enemies. This is a supreme test of our character.

Jesus' phrase "Love your enemies" is quite certainly the most distinctive teaching the world received from his lips. Those who successfully undertake this immensely challenging task, and who have forgiven their hostile neighbors from their hearts, achieve the final goal.

The point of entry for seekers into the Kingdom is not a mere tally of accumulated good deeds. It goes a lot deeper than that. Our initiatives for good, and the good we have actually accomplished, are a part of the total effort leading people to give and accept forgiveness and thus to be open to God's own forgiveness and bountiful mercy.

Summary

Jesus underscored three central convictions:

1. The will of God can only be totally fulfilled when every human individual honestly has a dominant desire and sense of urgency to seek personal wholeness.
2. Human life is significantly more satisfying for every individual who adopts this training and achieves its goals of openness, helpfulness, and forgiveness toward all other people.
3. Human society is capable of reaching its God-ordained destiny of social justice and peace, with true happiness and fulfillment becoming available to all people in the earthly Kingdom of God.

Nowhere in these few authentic words, coming down to us from his years of teaching, is Jesus seen creating an image of his own importance or divinity, or founding a church, or even starting a system of philosophy by which life's issues are to be judged. His incisive teaching, drawing strongly on the rich heritage of Judaism, is simply aimed at training the individual to be fit for the great race, the marathon of human life, and to achieve the goal of the race: participation in God's Kingdom here and now.

The metaphor of the race comes from Socrates. I don't suggest it was also Jesus' concept, but it is interesting to note that one of his followers, the anonymous author of the *Letter to the Hebrews*, used the metaphor and wrote: "We should…keep on running steadily the race we have begun." (Heb 12:1)

In the process of building up the reputation of Jesus, it appears that his followers in the fledgling Christian church resorted to following their own agendas and neglected to promote adequately his basic instruction. In his book of essays *What's Wrong with the World*, English Roman Catholic sage G. K. Chesterton commented: "The Christian ideal has not been tried and found wanting. It has been found difficult and left untried."

So it is for anyone today who is able to receive Jesus' central teaching as a message of clarity and purpose to turn it into personal action. Those who hold the opinion that Jesus is the divine savior of the world have a triple duty to try to follow his instruction, as they have never tried before, for God's sake and his, as well as for their own.

PART II
THE COACH'S WORDS OF WISDOM

The following account of Jesus' teaching is divided into thirteen sections, his words being interspersed with my commentary. The sections follow his dominant themes, exploring the nature and purpose of the Kingdom and how we are to work for its fulfillment in human society.

For simplicity, Jesus' phrases "the Kingdom of Heaven" and "the Kingdom of God" are translated "the Kingdom" throughout this section. Looking forward to God's new and better society, his teaching on the Kingdom highlights what such a society will be like, and how ordinary people can become its citizens.

Readers may wish to read straight through this section to receive the full impact of the teaching. Further reflection on the text may be helped by reference to the detailed notes printed in Appendix I at the end of the book. These are arranged in order by subject heading and the number of the saying. They also provide biblical references.

There is no known order to Jesus' sayings, so I have presented them in thematic groups to lend coherence to their message. The paraphrase of the original Greek is my own. Some passages have been placed together for the sake of clarity. I have labored to convey Jesus' thoughts as we have them recorded in the original Greek text.

The Kingdom

Jesus' Prayer

We start our study with the best-known example of Jesus' teaching: the prayer he taught his disciples. In this edition it is briefer than the version most Christians say in church, and much shorter than the original rabbinic prayer, which is noted fully in Appendix I
.

(Saying 1)
Father, may your name be sacred.
May your Kingdom come.
Give us each day our daily bread.
Forgive our debts as we have forgiven our debtors,
and preserve us from temptation.

This prayer, contained in the gospels of Matthew and Luke, is truly at the heart of Jesus' message. He believed passionately in God as a close and intimate parent. Jewish rabbis had started using the phrase "Our Father" in their prayers by that time, but Jesus used the intimate family form of the word—Daddy—implying absolute affection and trust. However, balancing familiarity with reverence, the prayer also declares that God's name is to be sacred, as was commanded in the Law of Moses.

The desire is then expressed that the Kingdom ordained by God will eventually come into existence. The whole teaching that follows has the single purpose of instructing Jesus' students in those principles of life they must adopt personally in order to ensure that the reformed society of the Kingdom is fully established on earth.

The request for daily bread is more complex than it appears at first sight. The first idea is that the phrase may refer back to the divine gift of *manna* to the Jewish people when they were starving in the desert. Each morning, according to the story (Exodus 16:14-21), an edible substance appeared in the fields, which was found to be nourishing. It did not keep fresh for very long, however, and each day a new supply had to be gathered. Thus, the idea that God constantly renews our supply of food is linked with the thought that his bounty meets our needs, enabling us to live from one day to the next without want.

The second idea relating to this request for bread is spiritual in overtone. Matthew's gospel may have recorded the saying, "Give us our bread for tomorrow." This reminds the petitioner of that Tomorrow which is life beyond the grave.

The prayer then speaks about the forgiveness of our debts owed to God, and our forgiveness of other people's debts owed to us. People at that time were used to the dual idea of forgiveness for debts or for sins. When Jesus of Nazareth first spoke the prayer, using his mother tongue of Aramaic, he probably used a word that had the double meaning of Sins and Debts. The idea of wrongdoing is involved, but the thought behind these words is that if we harm another person we are also committing an offense in God's sight.

The prayer ends with its most difficult phrase. Perhaps because of this difficulty, some scholars think it has been added to Jesus' original words by church leaders who were concerned when followers started falling away from the young Christian community. But in the teaching that follows this prayer, Jesus clearly outlines those habits and attitudes that his disciples must abandon if they are to live according to his Way. It is reasonable to think that a prayer to save us from temptation would apply to that situation. There is a further Jewish interpretation of these words that asks God to preserve us in the hour of final judgement of the world. It may be that Jesus had that thought also in mind: for two such meanings to exist side by side is typical of his style of teaching.

So, in this prayer Jesus is looking forward to a renewed society, instigated and inspired by God, in which human behavior will be reformed and people will be able to live together in happiness and harmony. The prayer requests that in the brave new world of God's Kingdom:

- Those things we hold most dear will be honored.
- We will work together for a new social order.
- Hunger and poverty will be abolished.
- Evil behavior will be put right and erring people forgiven.
- God will help us through the difficulties of life.

See also the notes in Appendix I

What Is the Kingdom?

Having spoken about God's Kingdom in his prayer, Jesus continues with an impression of what the Kingdom is like. In these passages and throughout the rest of his teaching we discover a strong sense of the temporal. The Kingdom is an earth-bound society created by people who have the right attitude toward life. It also reminds us of the eternal and loving will of God, bringing unity of purpose between what is going on here and now, on the one hand, and what will happen to us when life on earth is over, on the other. Despite this, we must not miss the Kingdom's essential earthiness. Jesus' teaching is clearly about the job we have to do here and now. In this he draws from the practical tradition of Judaism that identifies with great detail the daily steps men and women should take to be in harmony with the divine law. It is God's will that we should seek to bring about the renewed society of the Kingdom within our own lifetime. This challenge fills Jesus' message with its tremendous sense of urgency and purposefulness.

(Saying 2)
Don't stop the children from coming to me. The Kingdom belongs to childlike people.

We have to be careful to think of the teaching of Jesus of Nazareth in terms of how people in his own time would hear it. This saying, that children are the type of people to whom the Kingdom will belong, is not a sentimental idea but a religious comment:

- Children were seen in those days as possessing innocence or purity. Older people could find such virtue only as a result of God's forgiveness.
- Children are small and know it. Older people must cultivate an attitude of humility before God.
- Children are trusting. Older people must view God with confidence, to feel safe in God's merciful loving-kindness.

Christianity has often associated the idea of trust with that of our mental acceptance of specific beliefs. But this is a matter of emotional rather than intellectual response. It is not the mind's assent to religious propositions that Jesus is talking about, but the heart's child-like relationship with the God of love.

(Saying 3)
The Kingdom is like a woman who took yeast and kneaded it into fifty pounds of dough until it had risen completely.

The Kingdom is the risen dough, not the yeast. It is easy to get this idea the wrong way round. Jesus sees the renewed human society growing to fruition through the activity of ordinary people (the yeast). Thus the woman in Jesus' parable is involved in working for the expansion of the Kingdom.

(Saying 4)
It's like when a mustard seed, which is the smallest of all seeds, is planted. It grows into a large plant and becomes a shelter for the birds.

In the same way, it is the fully grown bush, not the tiny mustard seed, that represents the Kingdom. Its miraculous growth is the process in which we are involved, but here Jesus looks at the end result and refers to a contemporary metaphor of a bush or tree giving shelter to birds as being like a large nation with dependent states. The Kingdom will be a powerful force for good, and groups of people will find shelter within its sphere of influence. It is likely that Jesus hoped the Jewish people would be the first national group to embrace the concept of the Kingdom, and that they would promote the idea to all the nations and ethnic groups throughout the world.

(Saying 5)
The Kingdom is like a shepherd with a hundred sheep. When one of them wandered off, he left the ninety-nine on the pasture and went to look for the lost one until he found it.

This brief parable simply shows a Kingdom in which each individual (the lost sheep) counts for something, however many other people (the flock) there may be in the fold.

The image of Christ (as the Good Shepherd) rescuing a sinner (as the lost sheep) is deep within the Christian psyche. But this picture of the Kingdom as a flock of sheep with its shepherd does not really raise the issue of salvation from sin. This is a later interpretation of Jesus' words by one of the writers of the fourth gospel, that the Teacher is himself the Good Shepherd.

See also the notes in Appendix I

When Will the Kingdom Come?

Here follows an enigma. There is no set timetable for the coming of the Kingdom. As Jesus makes plain, it is not even easy to tell how much progress has been made. The reasons for this are that the arrival of the Kingdom's renewed society is essentially a secret process, and that people do not know the signs by which the Kingdom can be identified. On the other hand, all will become plain in due time, even as the seeds' secret growth in the earth and the long, slow ripening of the crop end with the grain harvest's amazing bounty, visible to all.

(Saying 6)
The Kingdom will not come by your watching for it. You won't be able to say, "Look, it's here!" or "Look, it's there!" The Kingdom is spreading out across the world and people don't realize it is there.

The Kingdom is not a political system but a way of life. It spreads through our society because people adopt its principles as their way of living. Social change is not being forced on people. We see them freely deciding to live in a better way, and their personal renewal will permanently change the nature of human society as a whole.

(Saying 7)
Imagine the Kingdom to be like this: farmers sow seed in the ground. They go to sleep every night and get up every morning while the seed is sprouting and growing quite unseen. The earth produces the crop all by itself: first the shoot, then the ear, and then the ripe grain in the ear. Finally, when the grain has ripened, it's harvest time and farmers get out their sickles.

The seed grows quietly, secretly, by itself. The farmer's job is to sow and reap. Nature does the rest through its continuous and inscrutable processes. The growth of the Kingdom does not depend on people being organized into working groups. It depends rather on the loving God who has already brought it into existence, and the ever-fresh supply of divine love enabling the servants of the Kingdom to help in its outreach to all people. As it is expressed by countless individuals, the Kingdom increasingly will take root in society. As a result, society as a whole will be changed for the better. In this parable Jesus clearly sees the hand of God working through nature, farmer by farmer, field by field, seed by seed. What a reward for a little patience! How little human work is needed to produce a harvest! How little we as individuals need to do to bring in the Kingdom!

See also the notes in Appendix I

What Will the Kingdom Change?

It is remarkable that Jesus describes the Kingdom in many ways, yet he is not recorded as giving a single directly reasoned explanation of it. So we learn that God's generosity is found in the amazing fruitfulness of the Kingdom. But we are left to work out the implications of that statement ourselves. Jesus wanted his hearers to compare the benefits of living in a renewed society with what they knew about the reality of living in one that had not been renewed. We are used to judging our society for its harsh, self-centered social inequalities and its mean-spirited response to human need, so it is a challenge for us to visualize a better one.

(Saying 8)
A farmer went out to sow. While he was scattering seed, some fell along the path and was gobbled up by the birds. Other seed fell on stony ground where there was little earth. It sprouted quickly in the thin soil, but when the sun came up it scorched and withered because it had no root. Still more seed fell among weeds, which so crowded in that it remained barren. However, the seed which fell on good soil sprouted and grew to produce a crop; in some areas it had a yield of thirty, in others of sixty, and in others of one hundred times what had been planted there.

This harvest demonstrates a bewildering change from the norm. A good yield from crops in Jesus' homeland was about ten times the seed the farmers planted. Compare that with the yield in the story. In this parable the benefits of the Kingdom are represented by the overwhelmingly abundant crop at harvest time. Jesus is confident that God is creating a society in which people's needs will be fully met and their faults truly forgiven. Good and evil people co-exist in the world, but those with positive attitudes—embracing goodness, truth, justice, and mercy—will find spectacular results in their lives. In such a Kingdom our little impulses for good turn into major accomplishments, and our feeble efforts are rewarded beyond our wildest dreams.

(Saying 9)

Which one of you would hand his son a stone if he asked for bread? Or if he's wanting fish, who would give him a snake? If you mean-spirited people know how to give your children good gifts, how much more likely is it that your heavenly Father will give good things to those who ask him?

In the same way, Jesus has confidence that the gifts of God will be adequate for our needs. Our parent God cares for us in the same loving way as the best of us respect our own children's needs.

Both these sayings point to the underlying confidence Jesus has in the Kingdom, which he sees God is willing us to create on earth. If we do, we can be sure it will work successfully and will supply the personal needs we have in the course of our lifetime.

See also the notes in Appendix I

Values For Our Life

The Great Consolation

From his earlier, tantalizing and exciting description of the Kingdom, Jesus moves on to talk about aspects of our experience of living in a renewed human society. For those who are concerned about becoming involved in any fresh venture, his words are comforting and reassuring. God will not neglect or forget those who live in agreement with the divine plan. Indeed, under the loving protection of God, human need becomes much less threatening. We are assured that our genuine concerns will be addressed, as Jesus himself asked in the prayer with which we began.

From now on, Jesus' teaching is directed toward us and our personal lifestyle. By the end, we will become aware that he is asking us to change our whole attitude toward life. Eventually the course of instruction begins to make sense: that how we should choose to live our life now is how everyone should live. Bringing in the Kingdom is a revolution in the lives of all human beings, everywhere.

(Saying 10)
Happy are you who are poor: the Kingdom is yours!
Happy are you who are hungry: the feast is yours!
Happy are you who are crying: laughter is yours!

In their search for authenticity in the sayings of Jesus, the Seminar's scholars have reduced the famous Beatitudes to three simple phrases, yet these are absolutely central to the message. Jesus sides with the poor, the hungry and the oppressed. Does that mean he believes these kinds of people are the only fit candidates for the perfect society? By no means! It is not that Jesus is commending poverty, hunger, or woe, but he is claiming that within a truly reformed society such blights on human life as these will be put to an end. For those in trouble, adequate support will be provided. It is the will of God that the Kingdom should be a place not only for the self-sufficient but also for those who previously could not help themselves. While people who have been brought low will be raised up by a caring society; those who are rich, well fed, and content, will be challenged to respond generously to the needs of others. All those who do so respond will discover an enduring psychological benefit in their own lives.

(Saying 11)
How much do sparrows cost? A penny each? Yet not one will alight on the ground without your Father's knowledge! As for you, every one of the hairs on your head has been counted. So do not be fearful: you are worth far more than a flock of sparrows.

To reinforce this message, Jesus uses the illustration of common sparrows that were sold at rock-bottom prices in those days for their tiny scraps of meat. He sees God as caring infinitely more for individuals than for these little creatures. The Kingdom stands for the dignity and worth of all people, irrespective of their status or condition.

(Saying 12)
Do not worry from morning to night about your life—what you're going to eat and drink, or how to find clothes to put on your body. There is more to living than food and clothes. See the birds: they don't plant crops to harvest and gather into barns, yet your heavenly Father feeds them. You're worth more than the birds! Can any of you add a single hour to your life by worrying? So, why worry about your clothes? See how the wild flowers grow—they don't labor or spin, but I tell you, not even Solomon in all his splendor was ever robed like one of them. If God decks out the meadow grasses, which are here today and used to fuel the oven tomorrow, won't he care much more for you, though you trust him so little?

Physical and emotional simplicity and reverence for life's gifts are basic to Jesus' teaching. He does not see any real necessity for large personal wealth, which can get in the way of true maturity. Our attitude must be one of a simple lifestyle and a simple trust in goodness. His illustrations deliberately make use of fragile subjects, birds and flowers. He reminds us that human beings also are fragile—here today and gone tomorrow—while the purposes of God go on for ever.

See also the notes in Appendix I

Our Basic Attitudes

Now Jesus uses shock tactics to make his audience aware of the seriousness of the mission on which he is sending them. His point is that our work to bring in the Kingdom will be a costly matter, demanding our total commitment. With one verbal hammer blow after another, these sayings reinforce a single, basic message. If we want to achieve our goal of bringing in the Kingdom, we must be ready to make that objective more important and more urgent than anything else in our lives.

(Saying 13)
Those who try to preserve their life will lose it, but those who lose their right to life will keep it.

First, we must change radically. We must exchange the person we have become for the person we want to become. It is our style of living, those things we stand for, and the personality we have cultivated in the past, which we have to surrender for the sake of the greater goal. (The idea of losing one's life by martyrdom is a later idea, made in light of Jesus of Nazareth's crucifixion and as a result of the persecution of the young church's leaders, many of whom were put to death.)

(Saying 14)
Try your hardest to get in through the narrow door. I tell you, many will attempt to do it, but will not be able.

This is the idea of the road less traveled. We need to choose the way into the Kingdom that involves a measure of self-control. If we are to achieve our goal of inclusion in the renewed society, we must avoid self-centered choices, both in our ethical behavior and in our attitude toward wealth.

(Saying 15)
Any who come to me and do not hold less dear their father and mother, wife, children, brothers, sisters, and

even their own lives, cannot be my disciples.

We need to re-examine the values given to us by our family and friends and, if necessary, be willing to take a different approach to living from the one we were taught in our youth. In thinking out a new way of life for ourselves, we must be prepared to risk leaving loved ones behind as we modify our behavior and make new and wider contacts among our fellow citizens in the Kingdom.

(Saying 16)
Let the dead bury their own dead: you must go out to announce the Kingdom.

We have to make a clean break with those people, lifestyles, and ideas that we have come to reject. We cannot go on finding reasons, even plausible ones, to carry on as before. Funerals were held on the day of death, so the call is for immediate action.

(Saying 17)
The Kingdom is like treasure buried in a field. When people find it, they cover it up again and excitedly go to sell everything they own to buy that field. The Kingdom is also like a dealer looking for beautiful pearls. When he finds a truly priceless specimen, he disposes of his whole inventory to buy that one pearl.

We must be prepared to get rid of everything in our life that stands in the way of our achieving our goal of becoming part of the Kingdom. This can be a joyful task, because we are not so much giving something up as setting out with a new vision to achieve personal fulfillment.

(Saying 18)
A city on a hill cannot be hidden. No one lights an oil lamp to hide it under a basket. It's put on a lamp stand where everybody can see its light.

Just as people cannot miss seeing buildings on the top of a hill, and just as lamps were made to shine brightly in a home, so we must be ready to work openly for reform in full view of our family and friends, who will then have an opportunity to understand our vision of being involved in a reformed social order.   See also the notes in Appendix I

Giving Up Power and Wealth

This instruction sets Jesus apart from his generation and many Christians in the modern world. Not only did he see people's habits and associations of a lifetime spent seeking wealth as a potential block to their wanting involvement in the Kingdom, but he was very concerned about the effect of wealth and power on their character.

He saw how difficult it was for people to have pure motives and sincere actions while living lives preoccupied with money and possessions. The dream of wealth must be for the community as a whole and not for any one individual (saying 8). Should a person achieve great wealth, Jesus demanded that it should be put to use in the community to uplift those who are in real need.

(Saying 19)
I am convinced that it is very difficult for the wealthy to become part of the Kingdom. It is easier for a camel to squeeze through the eye of a needle than for a rich person to be in the Kingdom.

This is a stark statement. Jesus sees that selfish concern to preserve wealth makes it hard, most likely impossible, for those with many possessions to become participants in the Kingdom.

(Saying 20)
If you have money to spare, don't invest it but give it to someone who cannot return it to you.

Instead of engaging in self-centered investing, we should be seeking to invest in genuinely needy human beings.

(Saying 21)
Whenever you give to charity, do not let your left hand know what your right hand is doing.

Gift giving must be kept absolutely secret, lest the one who gives to another derive personal advantage from the activity. Philanthropists should count the cost of their activity as little as possible, for thereby they will encourage their acts of giving to become habitual.

(Saying 22)
No one can serve two masters equally. A slave either loves one and hates the other, or is attentive to one and despises the other. You cannot serve both God and wealth at the same time.

Our ethical purity of purpose is compromised if we are in love with our material possessions. Jesus does not give any room for us to doubt his conviction that individual wealth is a hindrance to a society where people are meant to achieve equality.

(Saying 23)
There once was a man of great wealth. He said, "I will use my money to plant, reap, and fill my barns with produce, so I can have everything I need." These plans were dear to his heart, but the same night he thought about them, he died.

Although his success as an investor was not questioned, the rich man was seen as being poor in human terms because his thoughts were so entirely centered on his investment strategies. He had lost a sense of balance between his life's goals and his belonging to the human society.

(Saying 24)
Pay Caesar what belongs to Caesar, and pay God what belongs to God.

Jesus accepts the need to conform to the rule of civil law, but points out that there are opportunities to achieve higher purposes. The practical test is that we should accept things society obliges us to do, like paying taxes, but we should take advantage of every opening given us to bring fairness, justice, and freedom to other people.

See also the notes in Appendix I

Personal Qualities

Shrewdness

After hearing the call by Jesus for substantial personal sacrifice, the teaching that follows may come as something of a surprise. At first sight, the sayings about shrewdness seem to be directly opposed to the requirement to give up power and wealth. But historically the balance is quite appropriate. Forgetting this teaching, people have felt they had to be "unworldly" to truly follow Jesus. Over the centuries the retreat of a multitude of the faithful into seclusion is an example of how far this teaching has been ignored.

These passages actually tell quite another story—Jesus is calling for involvement in the world, in whatever situation we may find ourselves. He paints tough examples in which ordinary people are called upon to be shrewd. To drive home his point he uses other people's failures to illustrate our opportunity.

(Saying 25)
Be as sly as a snake and as innocent as a dove.

We have to reconcile our inner nature (being as innocent as a dove) and the street-smart qualities life demands. Examples follow of what that means in practice.

(Saying 26)
If you are about to appear with the plaintiff in a lawsuit, do your best to settle with him out of court, or he may drag you before the magistrate, who may turn you over to the jailer to throw you into prison. I promise, there you will stay until you have paid the last penny.

We must take care to conserve our personal resources so that we may maintain our place in the world. The Kingdom is not built by idealists or by timid people but by those with a clear view of their real situation.

(Saying 27)
A man going on a trip called his three slaves and entrusted them with his money. Before leaving, he gave each ten silver coins, telling them to trade with them. The first went out and put the money to work, doubling his investment. The second man also increased the money he had been given. But the third man dug a hole and hid his master's silver in it.

After a long time away, the master returned to settle accounts with the slaves. The first told him, "Master, you gave me ten coins. Look, I've doubled them for you!" His master congratulated him, "Well done! You are competent and reliable. You have been trustworthy with a small sum; now I shall put you in charge of a large sum."

The second told him, "Master, you handed me ten coins. Look, I made you another five!" His master congratulated him with the same words.

The last who received the money reported back, "Master, you drive a hard bargain, reaping what you do not sow and gathering what you do not winnow. I was afraid, so I buried your money in the ground. Look! Here it is!"

His master responded to his words, "You frightened and incompetent slave! So you know that I reap what I don't sow and harvest what I don't winnow? You should have taken my money to the bank, so I would have received interest on it when I returned. Take the money off this fellow and give it to the one with the largest sum."

As employees, we have to face our employer's demands for quality performance. If we respond in anger, or unsure of our ability to cope, we will probably fail. Courage, and a commitment to work effectively, are required of us. Jesus is consistent in his attitude about money. He knows that we live in a real world. Tackling the demand for common-sense money management has nothing to do with making the accumulation of wealth for its own sake a personal goal.

(Saying 28)

There was once a landowner whose estate manager was accused of squandering his property. He called for the man and said, "What's this I hear? I want a full account of your management—your job is on the line!"

The manager said to himself, "What am I to do? Master's going to fire me. I'm too weak to dig ditches and too proud to beg. But maybe there is still something I can do, so doors will open for me when I've been dismissed as manager!"

So he called on each of his master's debtors in turn. He said to the first, "How much do you owe my master?" The man replied, "One hundred barrels of olive oil." So he said to him, "Here's the deal: if you can settle now, I'll make it just fifty barrels." And he said to another debtor, "How much do you owe?" and was told, "A thousand bushels of grain." The manager told him, "Pay your bill now and I'll settle for eight hundred."

The master applauded his untrustworthy manager's shrewdness.

Even when we are under suspicion of doing wrong, we still have opportunities to use our skills. We are the best people to look after ourselves. In the story of the dishonest servant, it is not his lack of trust, currying favor with the debtors at his master's expense, but his business acumen that is regarded with approval by his master.

Jesus sees us all living with challenges, battling against the odds, wrestling with our own faults and inadequacies. He believes we have to be tough enough and shrewd enough to do the best we can, providing we do not lose the inner quality of caring for others which makes us fit for the reformed society of the Kingdom.

See also the notes in Appendix I

Persistent Patience

We now bridge the gap between being shrewd on the one hand and transparently honest on the other. Persistent patience is a kind of shrewd honesty. Society will only be perfected when people are brave enough and care enough to batter down the doors of injustice. Apathy in the face of evil can lead to great injustice, as Dr. Martin Luther King, Jr. pointed out during the Civil Rights struggle. Apathy and disdain for justice were the faults of the magistrate, and apathy toward his neighbor's need was the fault of the sleepy friend. Both were convinced in the end that they had to do something because of the honest need and the persistence of the other person. There is a kind of humble shrewdness in persistent patience.

(Saying 29)
Ask—it will be given to you.
Seek—you will find.
Knock—it will be opened for you.

Persistence in making our just claim is the right way to get what we really need. Another way of expressing these simple sayings is: "Go on asking, go on seeking, go on knocking." Jesus recognizes that society will not be transformed only by strong people taking action. The weak who need help must become involved and create change by asking for the assistance they need.

(Saying 30)
In one town there was a magistrate who had no fear of God and did not care about other people. But a widow from the town kept appearing before him, demanding he give his judgment against her adversary in a case she brought to his court. He refused for a while, but in the end said to himself, "I don't fear God and I don't care about other people, but because this widow keeps on pestering me, I'll decide in her favor or she'll wear me out with her constant demands!"

The poor widow, who never stopped trying to get justice, eventually won the day, wearing out the unscrupulous magistrate's resistance to her request. Weakness is not a barrier to success. The implication is clear: if she can do it, so can we!

(Saying 31)
Suppose you go to a friend in the middle of the night and ask, "May I borrow three loaves? A friend of mine

has just arrived on a journey and I haven't a scrap to offer him."
Then suppose he replies, "Do stop bothering me! The door is locked and my family and I are in bed already. I can't get up and give you anything!" Let me tell you, even though he won't get up out of friendship to give you anything, he certainly will get up and give whatever is needed, because you were not ashamed to ask.

The man who was not ashamed to pester his sleepy friend was calling on a strong social requirement to be hospitable to visitors. We can use social norms to win people's co-operation and their respect.

The shrewdness of our actions is demonstrated by our persistence; the goodness of our actions is found in our transparent patience. By acting in this way we show that we understand the frailties of those with whom we live, and make a sound judgment about how we should maintain our relationship with them.

See also the notes in Appendix I

Honesty and Integrity

Building on his call for shrewdness and persistent patience, Jesus moves to the demanding issue of inner motivation. He teaches that our need is to have a genuine childlike innocence in our relationship with God. Those who are dedicated to the Kingdom must go on striving to develop wholly integrated personalities. Such personal wholeness is essential for their success in working to bring into existence a reformed human society. We can only effect real social change honestly.

(Saying 32)

Grapes are not picked from thorn bushes, nor figs from thistles.

The things we do each day will clearly show to people the inner qualities we possess. Sweet results, like grapes, do not come from those with evil characters, like thorn bushes.

(Saying 33)

Salt is tasty, but if it loses its flavor how can it become salty again?

We must not allow our enthusiasm for high ethical standards, and our desire to live and work for the good of all, to drain away through neglect.

(Saying 34)
What goes into your mouth will not make you unclean; what comes out of your mouth makes you dirty.

The words we speak will show equally clearly the nature and purpose of our intentions. We are the creators of our words, even when we may simply be passing on what others have told us. We must be consistent in our promotion of the high ideals and values of the Kingdom.

(Saying 35)
Why do you see the speck of sawdust in your friend's eye, but fail to see the wooden plank in your own? How dare you say to your friend, "Let me get that speck out of your eye," when there is a whole plank in your own? You fraud! Pull the plank out of your eye first, and then you will see well enough to remove the speck from your friend's eye.

The way in which we criticize others vividly indicates what sort of people we think we are. When we try to reform others we inevitably throw a spotlight on our own personal inadequacies. Reforming society involves change of attitude. One of the greatest temptations of the reformer is that of judging other people negatively.

(Saying 36)
**Two men went into the temple to pray, one a Pharisee and the other a tax collector. The Pharisee stood and prayed silently in this way: "Thank you, God, that I am not like other people, thieves, crooks, adulterers—and most of all not like that tax collector over there. I fast twice weekly. I give tithes on all my profits."
The tax collector stood apart by himself and didn't dare to look up to heaven, but with a sign of despair**

muttered, "God, have mercy on me, a sinful man." Let me tell it to you straight: it was the second man, not the first who went home sensing he had been forgiven.

Jesus then puts these ideas in the context of our religious behavior. We may think that by our charitable and pious good deeds we are on the right track, but if the result of all we have done is that we bolster our high opinion of ourselves, our activities are worth little. He may have had in mind a saying found in the Talmud, a collection of teachings of the ancient rabbis: "In the place where the repentant sinner stands, not even the greatest saint can stand."

I see the Pharisee's flawed personality demonstrated by the soft judgment he had of himself and, on the other hand, by his harsh judgment of the tax collector. Jesus is talking about his vision of the spiritual life, and points to the means by which our human society can be put right. We cannot create the harmony of the Kingdom by standing in personal judgment of our neighbors. Whoever we are, we have real need of the loving mercy of the all-forgiving God.

See also the notes in Appendix I

Openness

Having in our mind Jesus' story about the proud Pharisee who rejected the trembling and repentant tax collector out of hand, we now find the theme taken further. If their work is to be successful, the servants of the Kingdom must open their hearts and minds toward all other people. Openness is not a passive state of mind. It demands personal action on our part and may prove to be very costly to us as a way of life.

(Saying 37)

Your heavenly Father makes the sun rise on bad people and good people, and sends rain on the just and the unjust.

At the heart of this teaching is the powerful Jewish concept of God's unlimited and merciful loving-kindness. All people, good and bad, are permitted to grow up together within the benevolence of God. The reason for social change starts with this fact of life. The Kingdom is where tensions between people are always being resolved and evil is always being confronted by good. The activity of the Kingdom's pioneers, with their common purpose of bringing goodness and justice to a mixed world of good and bad people, will eventually lead everybody to understand the peaceful aims of the Kingdom.

(Saying 38)
If you love only those people who love you, what's special in that? After all, even sinners love people who love them.

Jesus is especially good at undermining cheap grace—nothing comes easily in his view. When we don't risk anything in our personal relationships and stick only to the familiar crowd, we cannot expect to extend the Kingdom's sphere of influence or further our goals. That will only be achieved by our reaching out to people who are unlike us and do not share our lifestyle and our philosophy.

(Saying 39)
A man had a fig tree planted in his vineyard, but when he looked for fruit on it, he could not find any. So he said to his foreman, "Look, for three years now I have been coming here looking for fruit on this tree without success. Cut it down! Why should it be allowed to take the goodness out of the soil?"
In reply the foreman said, "Let it alone one more year, Sir, until I've dug round it and mulched it. If it fruits next year, fine, but if it fails, we can cut it down."

We should treat people as having social value, and we must give them adequate time to grow in understanding of the call for a renewed society. Here, Jesus uses the Jewish tradition of allowing a tree to have three years in which to bear fruit and suggests it should be given yet one more year. So, also, we must be patient and give people time to mature and to develop in goodness.

(Saying 40)
Someone threw a dinner party and invited guests. When the meal was ready the host sent his servant to tell the

Part II: The Coach's Words of Wisdom

guests, "Come, everything's ready!"
One by one, however, they all began to make their excuses. The first said, "I recently bought some land and need to inspect it; please excuse me." Another said, "I have purchased five pair of oxen, and I'm going now to try them out; please excuse me." Yet another one said, "I'm newly married and so I can't be there."
When the servant returned and told his master about the excuses, he was angry and told him, "Go into the streets and bring back anyone you can find to have dinner with me."

We may think that this story means that when people refuse our gifts or let us down in some way, we have a good reason to cut our losses by adopting the same spirit of generosity toward others who we know won't refuse us. We may even see this as the way in which we should handle people who reject the Kingdom and that we should embrace those who welcome its reforms. But Jesus goes deeper and looks at our preoccupation with matters of self-importance. God, the Host, welcomes to the banquet all those who accept their need for divine love. Inward-turning people exclude themselves by their indifference, while those hungry for love and understanding are welcomed.

(Saying 41)
The owner of a vineyard rented it out to some farmers to cultivate, so he could collect some of its crop from them. Later, he sent his servant to collect the produce due from the farmers. They seized the man, beat and nearly killed him, so he returned and told his master about it. The master said to himself, "Perhaps he didn't understand them." So he sent another servant, and the farmers beat him as well. Then the master sent his son and said, "They are certain to respect my son." Knowing he was the heir to the vineyard, the farmers seized and killed him.

This is a tragic story of misplaced trust. The son in this story is not

Jesus himself, a later Christian interpretation, but a metaphor for the Jewish nation as God's chosen people. As in his other stories with a twist in them, Jesus picks the anti-hero. At this time in history, landowners frequently oppressed their tenant farmers, so this tale of the tables being turned on a softhearted landowner would be quite remarkable at the time. There are dangers for anyone who tries to change the way people live. Some will take advantage of us and will use us for all they can get. Good and generous people do not lead charmed lives; they can be badly hurt on occasion. There is no promise made to the servants of the Kingdom that they will not get hurt.

See also the notes in Appendix I

Care for Others

Now we plunge into deeper water. Lest we have any lingering doubts that the quest to bring in the Kingdom demands everything we can give of ourselves, Jesus presses home two final demands. In this section we have the first, his instruction that we should adopt a totally caring attitude toward other people. If true openness can sometimes be hard to achieve, giving care to others is usually much harder. It requires that we are very practical in our relationship with other people, bringing to others the help we would ask for ourselves, were we in their place.

In this teaching we see the reverse of much of what is experienced as modern religion. It demands a costly response leading us to go without comforts, to get our hands dirty, to find ourselves in grim situations, and to be misunderstood for our generous attitude.

Once again, by inference, Jesus is pointing to a dynamic God whose merciful loving-kindness is expressed in practical ways, through the pioneers of the Kingdom.

(Saying 42)
Be happy, you who go hungry so that the stomach of someone in need may be filled!

We will find personal satisfaction in voluntarily choosing to deny our own needs for the sake of others.

(Saying 43)
Is there a woman anywhere who, if she has lost one of

her ten silver coins, will not light a lamp and sweep the house, searching carefully until she finds it? Then, having found it, she will ask her friends and neighbors over and say, "Let's celebrate! I've found the silver coin I lost."

The story of the lost coin is a metaphor for the thoroughness of the care we must give to lost people so that they may be brought back into a happy human society. The coin is a neutral object, not a wandering sheep, a delinquent son, or a preoccupied guest. The inclusiveness of the Kingdom is total—those who work to reach out and touch others are ordinary people living ordinary lives. But the result of their success is universal celebration!

(Saying 44)
There was once a man going down from Jerusalem to Jericho when he was mugged by a band of thieves. They stripped and beat him, then departed leaving him half dead.
A priest happened to be going down that same way. But when he caught sight of the man's body, he crossed the road in order to stay clear.
A religious scholar also came to the place, and on seeing the victim he also crossed the road to avoid any contact.
But a Samaritan traveling along the road came to the spot and was filled with compassion and went to help the man. He bandaged his wounds, pouring olive oil and wine over them. He lifted the man onto his own animal and took him to an inn, where he cared for him. The next day he gave two silver coins to the innkeeper and said, "Look after him until I get back. I'll reimburse you for your additional expenses."

Everyone easily identifies the Samaritan as an example of understanding and goodness, but we need to remember that Samaritans were most unwelcome visitors in Jewish territories in those days, and vice versa. Nevertheless, despite the current feeling at that time, Jesus turned this man into the hero of the story.

On first reading, Jesus seems concerned to show tolerance toward citizens of the neighboring state. He presents the Samaritan as a caring human being, in contrast to the self-centered local religious leaders. The issue is not only tolerance, however, but also a reminder how the religious establishment of his day missed the essence of true religion, the inclusive love of God. It must be a cautionary word for religious people of every age, including our own.

(Saying 45)
The Kingdom is like the owner of a vineyard who went out at dawn to hire agricultural workers. He agreed to pay them a silver coin for the day and then sent them to the vineyard to tend to his vines.
Coming out about nine o'clock, he saw other laborers hanging around the marketplace and he said to them, "Go to my vineyard, and I'll pay you a fair wage."
When he went out again at noon, and at three in the afternoon he did the same.
Finally, about five o'clock, he went out and found others loitering there and said to them, "Why have you been standing around idle the whole day?" They replied, "Because nobody hired us." He told them also to go to the vineyard.
When evening came the owner told his foreman, "Call the workers in and pay them their wages, starting with those hired last and ending with the first."
Those hired at five o'clock came and each received a silver coin. Those he hired first arrived thinking they would receive more, but each got a silver coin as well. As they took it they grumbled at the owner, "Those men you hired last worked for only an hour, but you treated them the same as us, though we did most of the work and suffered the heat of the day."
He replied to one of them, "Did I wrong you, my friend? The pay you agreed to was a silver coin, wasn't it? Take your money and go. I want to give those hired last the same I gave you. May I not do what I like with my money?"

The parable about the landowner sounds rather like a modern labor union dispute, but it is a searching analysis of motives. Unemployment in those days meant genuine hunger for the farm worker and his family. The employer was generous in taking on workers he did not need, in order that they should be paid, ensuring that their families would not go hungry.

In both of the stories in this section, the nature of the care given to others is seen to be demanding: the trouble and expense borne by the Samaritan and the bitterness of the disgruntled workers faced by the landowner. A renewal of our society will not come about unless we show the same degree of concern and care for others, regardless of the demands upon us which may result from our actions. God's amazing love is always "unreasonable."

See also the notes in Appendix I

Forgiveness

Jesus' final exhortation is that we should practice forgiveness. To enjoy a complete and satisfying life means to live always with a readiness to forgive other people. We need to give ourselves in this way not only toward those who are our declared opponents, who openly attack us verbally, and even physically, but also to those who simply hurt our feelings or do things we don't like.

Recognizing that the demand for a complete turnaround in our approach to living is a big one, Jesus implies that we are only being asked to live in a purely natural way, the way in which God has destined us to live. So, because it is God's way—full of understanding, mercy, and loving-kindness—it cannot ultimately fail to succeed.

(Saying 46)
Forgive and you will be forgiven.

This first saying takes us back to the opening prayer. If we forgive others, God will forgive us. Forgiveness comes first from God; even if other people will not forgive us, God can and will. In the Kingdom we must achieve mutual human forgiveness, because it is the bedrock of the new society that is being formed.

(Saying 47)
Love your enemies.

Jesus' central principle is rock solid. The root of the word "Love" is not sentimental, sexual, or easy. It is practical, costly, and has to do with welcoming, being hospitable, showing our good feelings to others, and not taking revenge. Since these things are not possible without a radical change of attitude, we must forgive even those people whom we call our enemies. There are to be no exceptions to our forgiveness. The unstated reason, once again, is that God is always ready to forgive people, however dreadful the thing they may have done. We find ourselves back again with Jesus' prayer, asking for forgiveness.

(Saying 48)
Do not resist an evil person. When someone hits you on your right cheek, turn the other side as well. When someone wants to sue you for your coat, give your overcoat away with it. When someone conscripts you for one mile, go two miles with him.

Having declared his principles, Jesus illustrates them. Apparent weakness is the hallmark of the forgiving spirit. We may actually allow others to take advantage of us, but by doing so we will show them how powerful forgiveness can be. This is Jesus' original and powerful concept of non-violent resistance.

(Saying 49)
The Kingdom is like a monarch who decided to settle accounts with his subordinates. To begin, they brought in a debtor who owed him millions. Since he had no way to repay, his master ordered him to be sold into slavery with his wife and children and all his possessions, so money could be recovered.
At this, the official fell on his knees before him and pleaded, "Be patient with me; I'll repay you in full."
Because the king was a compassionate man, he let the man go and forgave his debt. But as soon as he was released, the same man met one of his fellow servants, who owed him a trivial amount. Grabbing him by the

throat, the official demanded, "Pay me what you owe!"
The servant begged him on his knees, "Be patient with me; I'll repay you!" But he would not listen and he threw the man in prison until he repaid the debt.
Other officials who saw what had happened were really upset and reported to their master all that had taken place. Then the king summoned the man to appear before him. "You wicked servant," he said, "I wiped out your entire debt because you pleaded with me. Wouldn't it have been fair for you to deal with your fellow servant with the same generosity as I gave you?"

The story of the generous king and the mean-spirited debtor is not meant to quantify how far forgiveness should be taken. We should readily see that in Jesus' teaching our forgiveness of others is always on a much smaller scale than God's loving-kindness and forgiveness offered to us. But we need to open ourselves up for God's forgiveness of us to be effective. We must be willing to adopt a spirit of forgiveness based on our own need, showing our understanding of others' frailty by forgiving those who have hurt us.

(Saying 50)
There was once a man who had two sons. The younger one said to his father, "Father, give me my share of the estate." So he divided his property between them.
A few days later, the younger son collected his belongings and left home for a distant country. When he got there he lived extravagantly and squandered his inheritance. When he had spent everything, a severe famine devastated the country and he became destitute. So he found a job with one of the local citizens, who sent him into the fields to feed the pigs. No one offered him anything to eat and he longed to stuff himself with the carob pods, which the pigs ate.
Coming to his senses he thought, "All my father's hired men have plenty to eat, while I'm here dying of hunger! I'll go home and say to my father, 'Dad, I've sinned against heaven and against you; I don't deserve to be

called your son any longer. Treat me like one of your farm workers.'" So he got up and went home to his father.

While the young man was still a long way off, his father caught sight of him and was filled with compassion. He ran out to him, hugged him, and kissed him. Then the son said, "Dad, I've sinned against heaven and against you; I don't deserve to be called your son any longer..." But his father ordered his servants, "Quick! Fetch the best tunic and put it on him. Put a ring on his finger and shoes on his feet. Catch and kill the fattest calf; let's have a feast in celebration, because my son was dead and he has come back to life; he was lost and has been found." So they began the celebration.

Now, his elder son was out in the fields. As he got near the house he heard music and dancing. He called to one of the servants to ask what was going on and was told, "Your brother came home, and your father has killed the fattest calf because he's got him back safe and sound."

The elder son was furious and refused to go in, so his father came out and started pleading with him. But he retorted, "Look, Father! I've worked for you all these years; not once have I disobeyed your orders, yet you've never once given me so much as a kid so my friends and I could celebrate. But now this son of yours turns up, having thrown your money away on prostitutes, you slaughter the fattest calf for him!"

"My dear boy, you're always by my side," replied the father. "All that is mine is yours. But we had to be glad and celebrate. This brother of yours was as good as dead, but he's alive; we thought he was lost, but now he's found."

The parable of the Two Sons (called the story of the Prodigal Son) shows how intimately we have to deal with forgiveness, even within the setting of our family. The loving, forgiving Father in the story is like the all-merciful God. The tale ends without being wholly resolved. As in all issues of forgiveness, there is the question of how to interact with the forgiven. Like the elder brother, we have to decide what to do with those who have returned to society. We wait breathlessly for the elder brother to say something welcoming to his sibling, and find that it has been left for us to make the statement on his behalf.

We ponder over the elder brother's difficulty in finding forgiveness, both for his brother and for their father, whose perceived favoritism he despises. Then Jesus' message comes home to us. We are, much more often, not like the lost and wayward child but like the steady and unforgiving one. Family peace, indeed the peace of the whole world, depends on our forgiveness of other people, especially those we know most intimately.

This slim account of Jesus' training closes as forcefully as it began, centering on our need to be forgiving and forgiven. So a clear picture has been formed of the Kingdom: It is a society in which he requires us to be thoroughly dedicated to the cause, and open to other people in every way possible. In consequence of our commitment, the Kingdom's renewed society will be abundantly fruitful. In its atmosphere of forgiveness and mutual help, humanity will eventually find fulfillment and true happiness. See also the notes in Appendix I

Conclusion

I am certain Jesus originated the phrase *born again*, which appears in the Gospel of John (3:3). In view of the change a person must make to become a pioneer for the Kingdom, it is highly appropriate. Jesus implies that we must undergo a psychological rebirth in order to understand the depth of our personal commitment, as we take part in the work of the Kingdom. We must all change radically or lose the Kingdom's promised reward, the renewal of human society. It is such an incredible harvest that all will be amazed and no one will be left out.

A Summary of Jesus' Teaching

For those looking to summarize Jesus' teaching in everyday language, here are a few points based on this section of the book. For the sake of modernity, I have re-titled the "Kingdom" as the "Good Society." This summary draws on the original words of Jesus, but lacks their forcefulness. We must go to the Teacher and not his interpreters, for he provides the impetus we need to work for quality in our relationships and personal fulfillment in the growth of the Good Society. A summary is only a checklist. If we are serious, we will read the words of our Coach often, think about them in relation to our lives, and discuss them with other people.

1. Respect and revere the finest qualities you find in life, and look for their embodiment in a better human society. So that all human need may be met, commit yourself to overcoming evil with good, and to living in true harmony with other people.

2. Express child-like qualities of innocence, humility, and trustfulness as you work toward the goals of the Good Society.

3. See that the process of building a reformed human society has begun already, but the new order is destined to grow much larger and all-embracing. At present it can be found thinly spread across the world, but it will come into fulfillment when the time is ripe, working its way through people, good and bad alike, and astonishing everyone by its bountiful rewards.

4. Poverty, hunger, and distress will disappear in the Good Society because every individual will at last come to be recognized as possessing value and dignity. For this to happen, you must cease concentrating on the trappings of your lifestyle, and see instead that the ultimate purpose of the renewed society is to develop the potential for good in everyone.

5. You must be ready to turn life upside down. You must be ready to take risks, denying your perennial search for personal

advantage; giving heartfelt service to others; being true to the demands of ethical living, despite the pull of old affections; searching relentlessly for improvement in your relationships; and expressing your goals openly to everyone.

6. Privilege will hold you back from full involvement, so give it up. All must work together for the good of each individual. Give generously and sacrificially, and do so in secrecy to avoid selfish motivation. You cannot make wealth your personal goal, lest it sap your energy and distract you from your true purpose. Yet, remain shrewd in your daily business, retaining common sense when dealing with personal problems.

7. What is truly in your heart will be shown clearly in your life. What you say and do, and how you judge other people, especially those who are different from you, are the true measures of who you are. The truth about you will always surface.

8. Remain persistently patient in your honest search for self-fulfillment and for the Good Society. Be open, even to people who reject you. Give them chances, welcome them into your circle, and dare to trust them to do the right thing—knowing that your efforts will sometimes end in failure and personal loss.

9. Understand there is a deep psychological reward in self-sacrifice for the sake of others. Feed, rescue, and rehabilitate the needy, and supply their wants without trying to measure the worth of your generosity by their gratitude.

10. Your openness should be such that you always take the initiative in being forgiving and generous toward other people. Remember that if you are unforgiving, you cut yourself off from other people's forgiveness, and you will rob yourself of other people's affection if you refuse to acknowledge their generosity.

PART III
TURNING WORDS INTO DEEDS

Dreams and Utopias

NOTE: The term "Good Society" is used from this point in the book as a modern alternative to "Kingdom."

Making the Selection

It was a shock when I first read the selection of the teaching by the biblical scholars of the Jesus Seminar in *The Five Gospels: The Search for the Authentic Words of Jesus* (Appendix II). The idea of making a selection of the teaching found in the gospel narratives wasn't new to me, as I have explained, but it was tough to take some of the losses of familiar words I had absorbed as a child.

I know that these modern liberal scholars don't have a lock on the selection. Conservative biblical scholars may disagree with their judgments. But I am sufficiently convinced that the Jesus Seminar's pruned-down version of Jesus' sayings (the bulk of which is printed in this book) is more likely to be the core of his teaching than the longer version in the four gospels. It is patently clear that the evangelists edited their source material according to both their personal point of view and the needs of their local church community. They brought insights to the story of their Teacher, enlightening, encouraging, but also perplexing, subsequent generations. We who try to recapture the essential Jesus may possibly be less in need of their interpretation than people in their own day may have been.

Our ability to extract Jesus' original teaching from the gospels has been made both desirable and possible by the results of the generations of biblical research. We must remember that the sayings of Jesus recorded in the gospels were written down by editors who almost certainly were not present at the time, and wrote their accounts many years later. His words were filtered through several layers of personal opinion and contemporary church doctrine, and it has taken great effort to assess which of the recorded sayings might have been original.

In the end, I decided that the shock of losing favorite passages in the edited version was a useful experience. Now we have this material to consider freshly, as if someone had just said for the first time, "Here's what my teacher said; what do you think of it?" It is also good to consider the real setting of the life of Jesus, without the mystical overlay we have had presented to us for so long.

Jesus Attempts Reform

Opposition to both the brutal Roman occupying power and the Jewish religious leadership cost the outspoken Jesus his life. This may also be the result of his attempt to move the community in which he lived to embrace his concept of the egalitarian Good Society (Kingdom). Jesus hoped that change could be initiated by the activity of a spiritually renewed Jewish community throughout the scattered outposts of the Jewish nation all over the Roman world. At the time, Judaism was quite popular among foreigners as a strong, coherent, religious philosophy. It could have become a stepping-stone for a new, equitable, and peaceful society right across the Roman Empire. It might have led ultimately to freedom for the conquered peoples from the heavy hand of Roman oppression.

After Jesus' death, some of his followers took up his message, but eventually, in a different form, perhaps out of fear of further reprisals. Jesus, and not the Good Society of which he had spoken, eventually became the principal object of the young Church's proclamation. Emotion at losing the Messiah, or—as the Apostles insisted—at finding him alive, placed their spotlight on him as a unique person.

For a time, the new Christians gathered in small groups that seemed to reflect a willingness to fulfill Jesus' utopian message, but these cooperative communities were later abandoned as the movement grew larger and more scattered. Who Jesus was, and what he had done, especially evidenced by the resurrection story and by his healing miracles, became the substance of the Church's proclamation.

These two themes took over from his message of a reformed society. It became ever more obscured and diminished in importance as time went on. For the fascinating details of this development, read Burton Mack's study *Who wrote the New Testament?* (Appendix II).

Part III: Turning Words into Deeds

The Church Views Jesus' Teaching

Over the past century or so, the story presented by the Christian church has become less and less accepted by thoughtful people in the West. Doctrines that have no specific mention in the gospel narratives themselves, such as Martin Luther's "Justification by Faith Alone," and the highly detailed Roman Catholic dogma concerning the Virgin Mary's immaculate conception, perpetual virginity, physical assumption into heaven, and subsequent crowning as Queen of Heaven, have been questioned by many people who are believing Christians.

The Christian church sees itself, and is seen by others, as the sole trustee of Jesus' words and works. In a real sense, however, his teaching belongs to history and to the whole world. Whatever its claim, the church does not possess a monopoly on the interpretation of the teaching, and may even be inaccurate in its understanding of its purpose. The good thing about all philosophy or religion from the past is that it is open for everyone to view and for anyone to act upon. Once expressed, it belongs to you and me, not as experts, but as those who have the right to make sense of it the best we can.

This universal freedom of interpretation should be an important message for people inside and outside the Christian community. Nevertheless, the majority of church people act as if the call to have faith in Christ as a divine savior gives the church an exclusive lock on understanding Jesus of Nazareth's teaching and his way of life. Reinforcing this viewpoint, many church outsiders also tend to look at the church as unique, the only body truly able to tell us what Jesus stood for and how we should regard his ministry.

There is a small but growing body of Christian opinion, however, both clerical and lay, that sees the church as a very imperfect guardian of the words of Jesus. The main reason given is the way in which ancient dogma and past interpretation of the scriptures have held back the faithful from having a new look at the origins of the biblical narrative. After 2,000 years of Christian history, opinions among believers still differ widely on whether Jesus was the incarnate son of God or an inspired human teacher.

There are also painful differences of opinion about the reliability of the historic record of his life and teaching. In particular, interpretations vary as to whether Jesus' words were aimed mainly at the creation of an earthly Good Society under God's loving care, or at creating an opportunity for people to prepare for an eternal heavenly existence. In a sense both points of view may be true—Jesus' "Kingdom" may stand for a renewed society, which in its formation is also a model of God's heavenly realm to which we aspire, and for which we should prepare ourselves.

The Church has concentrated a lot of its teaching throughout the ages on the issue of people's spiritual needs, to give them spiritual preparation for a heavenly kingdom upon their death. In addition, the multifaceted dogmas relating to rituals and the personalities of the New Testament story have been a major church preoccupation. As a preacher in an African American church in Boston proclaimed in my hearing, "If you think the Christian gospel is all about having your 'pie in the sky when you die,' you are right!" I am glad to say that, despite his words, his own church has a strong and helpful social program to meet the many pressing needs of the local community.

Plain people, including many Christians, sense that the church may have spiritualized Jesus' teaching and ministry almost beyond recognition. In particular, the Christian assertion continues to be that salvation is for those who have faith in Jesus as God and Savior, and that our justification in the eyes of God is by faith alone (such faith being not an effort on our part but our willingness to receive the gift of faith offered by God in Christ).

Such doctrine contrasts sharply with the plain view that Jesus was a good man whose successful ministry healed and encouraged people and sought to lift them out of poverty and frustration by giving them the purpose of working for a renewed society. This work would lead not only to the renewal of the Jewish community, but also to the creation of a Good Society throughout the Roman Empire, owing its inspiration to the loving compassion of God.

In fact, Jesus' thinking may well have developed as his ministry progressed, beginning with his community and later, in response to interest by foreigners, broadening to include all nations (saying 4). That is not to suggest that Jesus conceived only a renewed earthly community. His prayer makes it abundantly plain that his disciples were to honor God, seek conscious dependence on God's goodness, and be forgiving, caring, and sharing in the manner of God himself, whose merciful loving-kindness he saw as the basis for all life.

I must leave the discussion of these theological and historical issues to others who, like the theologian Burton Mack, describe so interestingly the alternative streams of tradition from which we have received our picture of Jesus of Nazareth. Let it be enough for us to note that the spiritual teaching of the Church largely represents the work of Jesus' interpreters. So, in this book we will concentrate, simply and in a rather practical way, on his core teaching about the need to establish a Good Society here on earth.

Historic Utopias

From time to time, serious writers have created imaginary perfect societies, or at least ones different from their own. Thomas More, for example, wrote his book *Utopia* in 1516. There were popular literary treatments of the utopian idea, including the very different societies outlined in Jonathan Swift's satirical study *Gulliver's Travels*, and Samuel Butler's *Erewhon*, both pointing to the need for social reform.

The Buddha, many years before Jesus, reacted to the experience of sickness, evil, and death with teaching calling for the adoption of a new way of living based on Four Noble Truths and an Eight-fold Path of personal self-discipline. Other moral teachers of both the East and the West have tackled great human issues in their own ways. The sad thing in my mind is that—alone among the great moral teachers of the world—Jesus has suffered at the hands of his followers the ultimate penalty of being elevated to the position of a divine being, identified as one Person in the triune God. Buddhists venerate the Buddha and Muslims venerate the Prophet Mohammed, but in no way to the point of according divinity to either religious leader.

Jesus was a sincere itinerant preacher and spiritual healer, one of many such teachers at the time. He had popular success when he taught a new, open form of Judaism, primarily aimed at the poorer members of his own society. This took place at a time when the standards of the practice of Judaism may have slackened, possibly because of its popularity throughout the Roman Empire as a meaningful religion. Jesus' teaching was not especially original, but it was powerfully and humorously delivered. He thoughtfully called for significant changes to be made by people in their personal lives, in order to recreate their society with higher and more satisfying principles. Jesus' words survived because of the faith community that sprang up after his crucifixion.

Modern Utopian Ideas

Utopian ideas are still being created by sociologists seeking a new basis for social behavior and by politicians looking for new ways to refine government. The problem is that their ideal societies are not firmly based and demand more than most people are willing to give. Take the much-vaunted idea of equality, for example. People, especially men, seem to worship *inequality*. They pass tax laws giving many advantages to the rich. They idolize the lifestyles of the rich and famous. They elect to positions of power greedy people who are already saturated with privilege and wealth. They persist in treating women and ethnic minorities as inferior, and largely ignore the plight of hungry, children in single-parent families at the bottom of society.

Our generation worships power, whether it is political, economic, sporting, or sexual. We give preferential treatment to successful political leaders, wealthy tycoons, and the sports and entertainment stars of the day. People dream of winning a big lottery prize, or of collecting a large sum when a rich relative dies. Those who do succeed generally keep their capital and income for themselves and for a small group of relatives and friends—and see no reason why this should not be the most natural thing to do. Indeed, the so-called Great American Dream is based on the idea of people seeking to enter an economic meritocracy through their individual and largely self-centered efforts.

Ideas of how society can be improved are constantly with us, and each interest group works toward its goals in its own way. We find environmentalists working to preserve rain forests, the wilderness, rivers, and wetlands; to reduce pollution; and to conserve the earth's resources. Health enthusiasts concentrate on growing organic food, on exercise, meditation, positive attitudes, and balanced diets, all designed to promote health and longevity. Political and social leaders, architects, and urban planners labor in various (and often contradictory) ways to improve people's standard of living. But groups are often at odds with each other, as the broad spectrum of political ideology testifies. Even within groups dedicated to beneficial reforms there may be seeds of disagreement that can grow into a bitter harvest. One example: some physical fitness enthusiasts venerate the military, which is a direct cause of tremendous pollution and savage abuse of the world's resources.

Is a Good Society Possible?

At root, our difficulty with the ideal of a Good Society is that we do not really think it is workable. We are afraid that if we get involved personally in reform, the Good Society will end up demanding far too much of us. This is a self-made ceiling on our belief that any reformed human institution can make us truly happy. If we are seen to be social activists, we can find ourselves at the end of a limb, isolated, even laughed at for our attitudes. Reformers risk being thought odd and narrow-minded by their peers and loved ones. Worst of all, if as reformers we choose to work for no pay, we fear that we will fail to achieve our goal of being comfortably provided for in our old age.

Jesus addresses this dilemma by calling on our courage, saying that we must be prepared to put the search for the Good Society before everything, even ties to our family and friends (saying 15). We must give up everything that holds us back, like the dealer selling all to buy the perfect pearl (saying 17). Like him, in the end we will experience overwhelming satisfaction as our search yields the amazingly rich pearl of a thoroughly renewed human society.

Our fears are based on the knowledge that achieving true and lasting social improvement is incredibly difficult. If society is going to be truly reformed in order to make the world a better place for everybody, we will have to give up hedonistic practices and the accumulation of personal wealth for its own sake. Most of us feel that such a major change is improbable. This counsel of despair keeps people from reforming even themselves. Self-centered social attitudes are addictive, and nobody likes giving up an addiction, though we might do so from the fear of its consequences or when a more powerful person insists that we must. Most people are not willing to alter either their lifestyles or their social relationships, because they do not see the point of making any change which could lead to ultimate loss of comfort or social position, and, most often, because the reformer's ideas are insufficiently compelling.

An Earthly or Heavenly Utopia?

One effect of our not believing that human society can truly be reformed is reflected in our attitude about what happens to us after we die. We may feel unable to believe that an earthly Good Society can exist, but anyone can visualize that such perfection may exist in heaven. The Bible speaks openly about a New Jerusalem, and a whole bevy of pictures, carvings, books, films, mystical writings, and sermons support the idea that a perfect society does exist on the other side of the veil of death. Moreover, in the past sixty years, a huge amount of interesting literature has been published about people's near-death experiences and past-life regression to the "inter-life," speaking of sublime spiritual adventures they have enjoyed. Coupled with our society's well-known difficulty with the issue of death and dying, these witnesses have made it infinitely easier for us to think about after-life perfection than to believe that our human society can be transformed here and now.

This common attitude misses the point. Jesus shows that—both in the short and in the long run—a dynamic earthly lifestyle is much more satisfying than one spent focused on heavenly rewards. This totally new lifestyle is necessary for the achievement of the Good Society, a way of living we may actually enjoy during our time here on earth. It is sad that his highly relevant teaching about the *Here and Now* should have been so often sidelined by Church teachers, concerned with ideas about the *Hereafter*, that they have truly distorted his basic message.

What does <u>not</u> appear in this summary is talk about our going to heaven or receiving a heavenly reward. Rather, Jesus speaks of God's purpose for the world, God's care for people on earth, and God's standards for their lives here and now. He looks at the consequence of not being in a right relationship with God. Some in his audience might have accepted the idea of an afterlife, but it was a time when the powerful Sadducees taught that there was no life after death and no reincarnation. The heavenly reward is an interpretation of Jesus' teaching, based on his followers' writings. It appears in the Gospel of John and in Paul's letters, but it is not found in Jesus' core teaching. What he did say was that he believed in the abundantly fulfilling consequence of our becoming a part of the Good Society here on earth, and the opportunity to do so was real and immediate.

Reform Movements

The Church and Social Reform

In the past, those who have proclaimed a gospel based on good works have often been quietly put down by the faithful in the church as distorting its essential message. But Jesus' message belongs not only to organized Christianity but also to a world full of people who are literally dying because Jesus' practical remedy for the sickness of society has not been acted upon. The over-emphasis of mental assent to a spiritual formula, especially within the evangelical churches, and the demand throughout Christian history for detailed acceptance of church dogma, has had the effect of denying the centrality of the practical message of the Good Society.

Regrettably, the church fosters awareness of Jesus' practical earthly mission much less than he deserves. Examination of the actual content of modern Christian worship services points to the preoccupation of the church with ritual and dogma. In the Roman Catholic tradition, the virgin birth of Jesus, the immaculate conception of Mary his mother, teaching about heavenly salvation, the minutiae of Jesus' sufferings and death, the veneration of the cross and of Christian saints, and the presentation of the passion and resurrection stories occupy the vast bulk of the church's teaching. In the Bible Church tradition the great emphasis is on human sin and divine salvation, on rebirth into a personal relationship with the risen Jesus, and on the authenticity and reliability of the scriptural text. In both broad traditions the need to see Jesus as a divine, personal Savior draws from the Hellenistic tradition for the gods to have a personal face. It is remarkable that what the Church's "founder" actually said is confined to so very small a place in the church's calendar. It is as if many of the church's leaders were more interested in their own messages than his basic instruction.

An example of the spiritual put-down given to social reformers by the church was the withering attack by the faithful on the so-called Social Gospel. Many of the social reform movements that developed in nineteenth-century Christianity were motivated by the words of Jesus that we have in this book. The moderate Christian Socialists inspired many in their day, but they found the church unable or unwilling to give any great support. The followers of such teachers as Frederick Dennison Maurice were frustrated by their unfriendly Christian contemporaries and eventually found solace with others who were secular social reformers.

Christian Socialism

In Britain one example was the reforming movement of Welsh ministers and lay people in the little Methodist, Congregational, and Unitarian chapels in the Rhondda, the valley communities of the old coal and steel rust belt in south Wales. Oppressed by the working conditions down the mines and in the "satanic" steel mills, by the poverty of the over-crowded row houses, and by the heavily polluted environment, the preachers and their followers turned to the gospels' accounts of Jesus' reforming words for inspiration. These social pioneers persuaded and cajoled their followers into political and social activism.

At first the movement was church-based and spiritual, but soon it joined forces with other movements and the exponents of Marxist socialism to create the Labour Party in Britain. Eventually the broad socialist movement propelled Britain so far along the path of social reform that, on one occasion, thinking in terms of welfare programs and other social reforms rather than political party adherence, the Conservative party leader, Sir Winston Churchill, acceptingly remarked, "We are all socialists now."

Truthfully, Britain benefited from reforms made in that period. Health and safety at work and accountability for employment issues had been advanced. Social programs had helped people out of abject poverty, giving hope to young parents, better education for children, fiscal security for the aged, and basic healthcare to all. Legislation had led to pollution being reduced in the Rhondda and other bleak manufacturing areas throughout Britain, even if it had not yet brought full restoration to the surrounding desolate countryside.

Today the reform movement has largely outlived both its Christian and Marxist beginnings. It remains politically strong but centrist and essentially secular. The Christian church in Britain, having lost the social initiative, is viewed by the secularized mass of the people as being out of touch with the realities of modern life. That is not really true because, in the sparsely attended churches, despite the heavy and sometimes overwhelming cost of maintaining lovely, ancient buildings, the teaching of Jesus still inspires many good people to social action and to deeds of selfless generosity.

There remains in Christianity a huge latent power to grow the seeds of social reform. Indeed, it is a mistake to conclude that the church has abandoned the practice of encouraging loving and sharing communities, as some of its cynical critics would have us believe. The good deeds and warmth of affection that are the signs of the Good Society are to be found in all branches of the Christian community throughout the world. But, with one exception, the real drive of Jesus' vision is missing; that exception is missionary work.

Christian Mission

The historical fact is that Christianity has been an enthusiastic driving force behind many social reform movements throughout the world. Although the Jewish and the Sikh communities, for example, also have a distinguished record of creative social activism and the formation of fine institutions for the betterment of their people and the world, their efforts are less frequently publicized. In contrast, Christianity has been aggressively expansive. Bubbling with triumphal missionary zeal, it has attracted many of those most caught up by Jesus' practical teaching to take not only faith in Christ but also his message of good works and a new social order to the nations of the world. In consequence, clinics and hospitals, schools and universities, justice systems and well-regulated government services have been established in many parts of the world, with the help of missionary-led teams of workers.

There is a saying in missionary circles that "the church exists by mission as a fire exists by burning." That attitude is a testimony to the concept of the Good Society because so often the white heat of Jesus' practical caring work is centered on missionary movements, including rescue work in shelters for the homeless and hungry. Yet the relationship between many in the churches and their overseas mission projects can be uneasy. Mission demands money and sends to far away places some of the church's most highly committed younger members. For very many parishioners funding the provision of Bibles and church buildings abroad (comfortable and tangible gifts) is a safer, hands-off way of supporting the Kingdom of God than becoming personally involved in relationship-centered outreach.

I recall in 1969 being shown, by the assistant governor of the Tu Duc women's prison in South Vietnam, a collection of five hundred large, English-language bibles, given to the prison by an American church group. Valued by the devout Vietnamese Buddhist community as a spiritual gift, they were obviously unused. Two French-speaking Buddhist nuns who approached me later in my visit to Vietnam, asking me to explain the nature of the probation system set up by western nations' courts, were more in touch with Jesus' mission than the earnest Baptists who shipped crates of Bibles into the oblivion of the prison bookcases.

Capitalism and Communism

During the twentieth century, the world witnessed a giant struggle between competing philosophies, both of which had taken root in previous centuries. Both movements pursued their agenda for the improvement of society with such aggressive determination that, in the nuclear-armed standoff between the communist Soviet bloc and the western capitalist nations, the fate of the world itself hung in the balance. But it was a struggle in which both ideologies have proved to be woefully inadequate. Capitalism may have been proclaimed the victor of the Cold War, and because of the brutality and mismanagement of the Russian leaders, the Marxist dialectic has been disgraced, but the issue is not over at all. The world's huge problems have not been resolved, and many observers assert that, as the world's population has ballooned, hunger, poverty, and economic disparity have multiplied fast since the end of the Cold War.

History has a habit of debunking ideologies. World population growth and economic change have created the largest polarization of people ever, between the tiny minority of incredibly affluent and powerful people controlling the economies of the nations, and the vast majority in the world of poor, powerless people who are without any chance of betterment. Indeed, the reviled Karl Marx's assertion that polarization is an inevitable social development was not wrong, even if his revolutionary conclusions have been discarded. At the beginning of the 21st century we are worse off by far, in terms of global poverty, than when Marx sat down in the 1860s to write *Das Kapital* in the Reading Room of the British Museum.

Communists identified social polarization and the risks of a money economy, but failed to correct the problem despite possessing total control over their population. The fault lay in the greed and arrogance of leaders and the brutal inadequacies of the social model. Capitalism talks about people's dreams of climbing from poverty to wealth by dint of hard work, using the carrot rather than the stick approach to social reform. But the whole world knows that for everyone who manages to rise in personal wealth, ten thousand people worldwide sink further into poverty. Multinational corporations overwhelm democracies big and small. The global money economy is the driving force behind polarization of wealth and poverty. Half of the world's six billion people are permanently hungry, poorly clothed, poorly housed, and without economic hope. At the same time the small number of billionaires multiply their assets stratospherically. At one recent count, the world's top 200 (US$) billionaires had personal assets equal to those held by the one billion people who comprise the poorest in the world. Yet even this appalling figure gives no account of the trillions of dollars' worth of assets actually controlled by the 200 people in question. But there is hope for change; the spinning satellites, fast global transport and commerce, and intimate linkage of people via the information-saturated Internet all point to the oneness of the world community and our greater ability to effect social change if we want to do so.

Both communism and capitalism have the same flaw. They are about power and wealth. Communism seeks to give the people total control over the wealth of their country, but fails to understand personal motivation. Capitalism values individual initiative, but ignores corruption and greed. Both impose a remedy on the people. Jesus' approach grows answers from people's values and experiences, starting with shared experiences and aspirations. It's nothing like the great materialistic systems—and that's the point!

Jesus' Vision for Humanity

The Purpose of our Society

What kind of society do we really want to live in? What sort of true human satisfaction do we really crave? What type of human heritage do we want to leave for our children and grandchildren when we die, as surely we must? These are questions that flow from listening to the teaching of Jesus.

The instruction he gives in answer to our question is a mixture of both putting ourselves to the test and holding on to others for support at the same time. All individuals need understanding, support, fun, and most of all, love. Next to sips of water, it's what we all need most. Little babies in hospitals have died when the nurses were too busy to love them. There are millions of people walking around our world today in a mental fog, who died emotionally years ago because they were not truly loved by anyone. Jesus focuses on the support and acceptance everybody needs when he commends to us the work of renewing our society.

If we see the Good Society as a kind of holiness club, to which only good people can belong, we've got it absolutely wrong. If you don't believe that, re-read the message. Jesus was sure that the good and bad, the likable and unlikable people out there in the world, all inherently belong to the Good Society. They belong because working for reform, like running toward the finishing tape in the marathon, is a state-of-becoming for all of us. The renewed society is one that will work for everybody in the end, whoever they are and wherever they may be and whatever they may have done.

Essentially, Jesus' view of the purpose of life is that the loving benevolence of God is the basis of our relationship with our Creator and with all other people in our community. Standing on the firm rock of divine love, we are enabled to express our love for God by working in the Good Society that God has inaugurated. In this way we may come to understand and implement the reality of sound and healthy relationships. The Good Society's objectives are achieved as committed workers start living in true relational harmony with one another. His view is not political, like the Marxist blueprint, nor is it about personal and economic opportunities, as capitalism asserts. Jesus saw that the true dynamic behind lasting societal reform must always be the quest for personal relationships of purpose and quality. There is nothing more fundamental than that in the life of any society, whether primitive or highly sophisticated. So the qualities needed to bring about good personal relationships must become foremost in all our lives, or society will never realize its full potential.

The issues Jesus raises are not just about wealth and poverty. He pleads for an open, caring society of peace and justice. As Dr. Martin Luther King, Jr. pointed out, society must learn to judge people not by the color of their skin (their social difference), but by the content of their character (their social value). The brutal treatment of women and children in many countries, often encouraged by the cruel exploitation of their labor by big business, is an example of the desperate need for immediate global reform.

At such a time as this, despite the spiritualizing doctrines of the church and the indifference of a mass of self-absorbed people, Jesus' teaching offers a hope to the world that has been exemplified through the ages by the enormously effective lives of enlightened people from St. Francis of Assisi to Mother Teresa of Calcutta. Jesus reaches his point of greatest relevance when things are at their worst and society is sundered by economic polarization or war. G. K. Chesterton may have been fair in saying that Jesus' teaching had not been tried and found wanting but really had not been attempted. Yet Jesus himself said optimistically, "The Kingdom is spreading out across the world and people don't realize it is there" (saying 6).

That was certainly true in the life of the Hindu sage and independence fighter Mahatma Gandhi, whose doctrine of *Satyagraha* (Truth Force) bore a direct relationship with Jesus' Sermon on the Mount. We don't have to be Christian in order to work for the Good Society. Gandhi was a clear case in point, melding ideas into his philosophy from many religious sources, and from radical writers including Ruskin and Tolstoy. Since Jesus' words belong to the whole human society, anyone, of whatever religious persuasion or of none, may take them and join the work of bringing in the Good Society.

Perhaps Jesus remembered the Talmud's saying, "The righteous of all the earth shall inherit the Kingdom of Heaven," and foresaw people in their old age sitting in their garden, thinking with satisfaction over the things they said and did and the people they had helped in the past. Maybe he saw them, having first broken with the selfishness of past generations, at last enjoying the sense of the emotional and relational progress made in their lives, and the way their comrades had made similar progress and received equal satisfaction.

The first goal of the successful marathon runner is beating a personal time-barrier, which can lead to the goal of being the first to break the tape. Yet I believe that, despite their dreams of winning, the very finest athletes are less consumed by the desire to win than they are intent on using the challenge that other runners provide them to run the very best personal race they can.

The task Jesus sets for life is the way of personal fulfillment. After working to reform society, and having found a satisfying way of living, we will able to say modestly that the world may just be a better place because of our efforts. But let's get Jesus right. It is not only the fulfillment of the individual, but also the betterment of society as a whole, that is at stake. It is a fulfillment already here through God's reforming impulse.

Put it another way—what sort of society would you like to live in? What kinds of people are needed to help create such a society? Jesus' idea of a reformed society isn't a political blueprint; it is much wiser than that. No political blueprint will ever get it right because we will all still have to deal with people who are greedy, angry, obtuse, selfish, and cruel.

Communism started out with a passion to create a truly fair society. But its roots were in hatred of the rich and its method was one of violent revolution. The seeds of its self-destruction were there from the outset; the leadership was infected, so true social justice never had a fair chance of success. That's why communism failed. Despite its material successes, capitalism's road of self-interest, taken to achieve its objectives, provides the reason why it continues to fail as a means of making human society wise and fair in its treatment of every human individual.

Jesus saw clearly that individuals first have to change themselves or society will never change for the better. Capitalism and communism were destined to fail for that reason. People must get together in small groups whose members are dedicated to change, so that they can have courage to take up the new attitudes needed to reform society. Then, like the yeast spreading through the dough (saying 3), or the seed growing secretly in the soil (saying 7), in the end the change in human society will take place. The dough will rise into bread; the seed will sprout into a crop. And what a crop (saying 8)! If people really change, and their numbers have multiplied, then eventually society itself will change for the better.

The Good Society is founded on the belief that the global human society can be transformed from within by common people acting locally in accordance with their highest principles. This change cannot be engineered for society; it must come about spontaneously as individuals improve relationships and give mutual support and care to other people. This will only happen in those groups where the Good Society is seen as worth working for. It will never result from coercion to conform to a set of rules or laws, but only from the encouragement and example to do good in a consistent way, given by people with a deep inner desire to achieve that end.

Those who work for change in society will apply its principles first to themselves. They must undergo the self-discipline that leads to a thorough change of attitude and a personal commitment to a new way of life. For this to be so, those working for the Good Society will adopt the same level of unqualified trust in its success that can be seen in little children's relationship with their parents (saying 2).

Everyone will ultimately benefit from the social change resulting from this work of renewal. It really is possible for every person on earth to be given attention, care, and support. Initially, not every attempt will be successful. Not all the people who are involved will be wholly well, either physically or psychologically, so change will take time and effort. Yet all people can be offered understanding, forgiveness, and open acceptance, and can be challenged to give something back to society in accordance with their level of understanding and ability.

The practice of responsible personhood brings immediate psychological and spiritual rewards. Our openness toward others may be costly (saying 44), our forgiveness may be rebuffed (saying 49), our generosity may be unacknowledged (saying 45), but we will be the richer in self-giving of this kind. As we learn the methods of creating the Good Society we will be astonished by its flowering in our life and our circles of family and friends.

The Discipline of the Good Society

If the teaching of Jesus has been left untried, as Chesterton suggests, one reason may have become obvious from the brevity and simplicity of his message, extracted from the much longer gospel records and printed in this book. His core teaching has actually been quite difficult to find!

The simple message Jesus taught had been sadly obscured by the multi-layered additions and interpretations both of the first evangelists and of subsequent church teachers. Only as the patient detective work of biblical scholarship has finally yielded a sound selection of his core teaching has the clear message been able to get through. This stripped-down account of his teaching is one we can readily understand, even if it is very hard to put into practice. But we must also compare Jesus' teaching with that of other thinkers, both before and after his time, and those whose practical work was to take forward the society in which they lived.

The concept of the Good Society implies a judgment that every society can truthfully be measured as being "better" or "worse." For those who don't associate such ideas with doing the will of God, the idea of goodness is pragmatic. Their test is: "Can society ameliorate the lives of *all the individuals* of which it is composed?" If it is impossible to improve any life further, then society has truly reached its goal. The implication is absolute: the reformation of society can be complete only when all people are living with as much success and as much personal acceptance as they themselves may reasonably ask, and as others can lovingly conceive for them. In a perfect clock, each part works as it was designed so all can work perfectly together.

At the beginning of the third millennium after Jesus' birth, we may see that humanity has been taught valuable lessons by the science of Copernicus, Galileo, Newton, Darwin, Einstein, and many more great minds that have helped us to understand the nature of the universe and of human society. We have seen the rise of secular and religious humanism in social movements and in specific philosophies. Our attitude toward the ecology of the earth and our view of the cosmos now temper our judgments as never before.

All these developments embrace deep and serious discoveries that signal a significant evolution in human thought since the first century. Modern secularism is not a facile rejection of ancient theologies. Rather, it means leaving off the religious gloss that many want to have painted over their statements about life. It also involves looking, with Einstein, at the cosmos as constructed throughout of energy, not somehow divided into the supposed twin realms of the material and the spiritual, and pondering what such an idea may mean for the future of our faith.

Does this mean that in order to be honest we must either choose Jesus' God-centered view (as the Church asserts we should) or seek a different teacher? I do not think so. Look back at the marathon race idea. I chose Jesus of Nazareth as my coach because of his reputation as one who makes plain the way for people to prepare themselves for life's great trial of character. I saw him as able to unlock the secrets of my motivation. I did not believe that anyone, religious or secular, had ever expressed these things as deeply, as simply, or as well.

What is your motivation? Can we all have an equally valid interpretation of life, giving us strength to go forward to reach our personal goal? People have never successfully attempted the marathon without real inner motivation, nor have they run in such a race without also finding that motivation leads to self-discovery, and to the painful realization of what personal fulfillment demands. What is true of the great marathon race is true also of life. If we run the race of life only in order to please God, or only in order to build a better society, it will be a poor race. Runners have to cope with shortness of breath, with thirst, with weary limbs, and with paths climbing steeply upward. As we overcome difficulties, we discover ourselves and find out what really matters in the end.

Whether we are in fact a runner, or just someone trying to live life fully and well, we know that our motivation will demand all that is within us. We must change from what we have been and become focused and dedicated to our personal goals instead.

Seeking to find their motivation for the race of life, people come to the coaching of Jesus of Nazareth in a variety of ways—some expressing traditional faith, and others simply filled with the desire for a better society. They come from meditation and other forms of spirituality with a recognition that the universal harmonies they have discovered in the stillness also lead to perfection in the life of society, but will involve them in a good deal of hard work as well.

Just as the runner strives for a Personal Best, so we will find that the demand of Jesus' teaching is a challenge for us to do better than ever before in our relationships with other people. His teaching points to the ultimate satisfaction of well-tempered relationships in a well-tuned human society. He saw happiness breaking out in those societies where people put in a real effort to get relationships right. In the middle of a troubled, dangerous world, where greed, violence, and despair seemed to triumph, his vision was that there are always pockets of resistance, representing the emergent Good Society. And the experience of these groups of individuals, who are working hard at their relationships with their neighbors, is an encouragement for others to take the initiative and do the same.

Yeast Rising

Jesus of Nazareth saw that human society is capable of being transformed, but it will only be changed and brought to perfection when individuals submit fully to the self-discipline of creating sound and caring relationships with all around them.

There is no place for the self-absorbed loner in this message. Success depends on one person's inspiring another to get it right, working from personal convictions to a new way of life in the small group, then out with the people of that group into the next larger section of society, and so on, until all the dough has risen completely. As the first disciples of Jesus realized when they attempted to carry on his work, it is teaching that cannot be kept in a book or in a secret organization. Alas, because of pressures upon them they preferred to soften the message rather than face the intensity of its demand. That pressure, from within ourselves and from others, still remains a trial for us and for the success of the message today.

The message of Jesus is like a handful of yeast in a great tub full of dough, moving cell by cell throughout the mass, until all the dough has risen for baking bread (saying 3). It is a clear answer to the age-old impossibility of trying to reform society by political means. It is also the social reality behind the idea of Jesus' rising from death: not a body coming out of a grave, but a way of life moving from the small circle of a teacher's influence, in a far-away time and place, out into the modern world. And here in the world of our generation, where we need so very urgently to reform the way we live together, it is a perfect coaching for the race we must run together in the marathon of human life.

Excellence

The cry of billions in the world today is there in Jesus' prayer: "Give us each day our daily bread" (saying 1). Its fulfillment, in his catch-phrase "Happy are you poor, the Kingdom is yours!" (saying 10), is in the re-creation of our society to be truly more fair and loving. But how is it to be done? "You won't be able to say, 'Look, it's here!' or 'Look it's there!' The Kingdom is spreading out across the world and people don't realize it is there" (saying 6). We are immediately at the point of difference between Jesus and other social reform movements. The Good Society is not going to happen because of political organizations, church initiatives, broad social movements, or government edicts. These may be some of the consequences of the Good Society, but they are definitely not its wellspring.

Jesus points the finger at you and me, at our family, our friends, and our neighbors. Individuals will be working informally through little groups of friends, a tenants' association, a street community, a small village. Tiny units of committed people will create the Good Society. And where will they create it? Among themselves—no more and no less. This is not some kind of church missionary proposition; it is a call to ordinary people, religious and secular, for excellence in living together in the place where they are already. Going out to persuade other people may be one consequence of success in building the Good Society, but it is not the primary means by which it is created.

Jesus' key to social renewal is at a level that touches us personally. It will only happen if we ourselves are totally involved. The Good

Society cannot be our experience unless, first, we are committed to it. Other members of our family or neighborhood may create the Good Society for themselves, but that doesn't mean we will share in it. If we are not at one with the objectives of the Good Society we cannot be part of it. This is the reason why Jesus is very pointed on the personal level. The demand on us is total: "Which one of you would hand his son a stone if he asked for bread?" (saying 9). We are all engaged, much of the time, in giving short change to our nearest and so-called "dearest." Our expressions of anger are most likely to be heard within the four walls of our home. Violent men who hit their wives and children frequently will often not dare to hit anyone else in the whole of their adult lives. Scheming children try out deception on their mother, knowing she will softly forgive them, rather than on their teacher, who will not. We must face a very personal demand. The story of the two brothers (saying 50) pictures the elder brother shaking with rage at his wayward sibling who dared to come back and disturb the peace of the family. So very like the terrible rows that occur during public holidays when many families gather together only to snarl and fight from the moment they arrive until the time they go home.

Forgiveness is central to our relationships and demands a very practical turn of mind. At the core of social atrophy is our common unwillingness to be forgiving. Forgiveness is absolutely essential to successful, permanent social change. We sigh, "If only people could be made to be forgiving," but that's not the way of Jesus. We must be the people initiating change. We are the people who must practice forgiveness first so that others may see that it works (saying 18) and then try to follow our lead.

When you think about it, political philosophies do not have very much to say about individuals spending time and effort to make personal changes. Social reform is usually seen as a broad community affair, even a government-directed thing. If, as in capitalism, individuals take an initiative, it is for personal financial betterment; it is to pull themselves up out of poverty by dint of hard work. Capitalism does not care if the individuals involved in self-improvement are saints or swine. What matters in this philosophy is the reward for hard work, and amelioration of the living standards of the successful as an encouragement for others to do the same.

Wealth

The initiative Jesus envisions is not made for the financial benefit of the individuals taking part so much as for the benefit all around them. In the story of the self-made man licking his lips over his growing financial empire, and happily counting his personal assets on the eve of his sudden and unexpected death (saying 23), his real problem was that he had no concept of a relationship with other people. He was successful, but to what end? Looking at the Forbes 400 list of the wealthiest people in America, I found myself asking the question "why?" Why would people want to be so wealthy that they could not possibly spend all their money? You don't need a billion dollars to have a big house, an expensive car, and servants, let alone 30 billion. Is power the real objective of the wealthy, and money just the means to that end? Yet who gave them the right to be so powerful over the lives of other people? God? If they have, say, twenty-seven thousand people working for them, how do they know what their exercise of power in those workers' lives really means to each one?

The issue Jesus is raising is incredibly apt for our time. Maybe he isn't really against wealth as such; he is for truly good relationships and sees wealth as inevitably getting in their way. If the self-made man in the story had only built his empire for the good of society as a whole, his death (on which his estate might be transferred to benefit society), would have crowned his achievement. It would not have been the ruination of all his dreams.

Jesus sees wealth as the potential master of our lives. "You cannot serve two masters equally. You cannot serve both God and wealth at the same time" (saying 22). Maybe this saying is simply against our turning wealth into our master. Jesus' test is what we actually do with our wealth. If we are caught up with the love of money, for example, when we give to charity our main aim will be to feel pleased with ourselves at what we have done, and also to enjoy being flattered by others for our generosity. In other words our love of money is the veiled love of self. Conversely, Jesus declares that our giving should be so secret that we don't even know we've done it! That's of course a deliberate exaggeration. "Whenever you give to charity, do not let your left hand know what your right hand is doing" (saying 21). That way we ensure our sense of self-importance is not the real objective of our giving.

Was Jesus against wealth? He said, "It is very difficult for the wealthy to become part of the kingdom" (saying 10). He did not say wealthy people could never be a part of the Good Society, just that it was very difficult: so very difficult—like the camel trying to squeeze through the eye of a needle—that you could say it was impossible. Hope for their success could still be expressed, though, because there are many ways in which wealthy people can demonstrate that the love of money is not the controlling factor of their lives. One example is: "If you have money to spare, don't invest it but give it to someone who cannot return it to you" (saying 20). Put that together with the idea of giving to charity in total secrecy and you have a dynamic duo.

Giving

Philanthropy is the clue to a way in which the affluent can actually enter into the discipline of the Good Society. Their success becomes the means by which the whole of society is given chances for betterment. The old saying applies here, that giving a man a fish to eat is not as good as giving him a fishing rod and teaching him how to catch fish. What the poor need most are not handouts, which make them feel small. Pretentious people who like to puff up their ego by distributing largess often give handouts condescendingly to the poor. The poor need personal acceptance as equals, a warm home, food, education, fairly paid permanent work, and an opportunity to share in the caring life of the whole society.

Let us think up a scenario in which the wealthy people in an area club together to open a small factory employing the poor of the neighborhood. The factory would be modern, with good training courses, healthcare provisions, childcare for babies, and retirement pensions. And the sponsors might not be too troubled if the factory only just scrapes a profit, providing the dignity and comfort level of the poor people working there steadily improves.

Tzedakah, the Jewish term for charity (seen as the transfer of wealth), has at its root the meaning of fairness, or justice. Reflecting on the biblical verse, "Happy are those who use insight when giving to the poor" (Psalm 41:2), Maimonides, the twelfth-century Jewish sage Rabbi Moshe ben Maimon, established an interesting ancient formula for judging the way we give our charity. Maimonides' eight-step ladder of giving starts with the worst sort of giving and progresses to the best:

- Giving in a begrudging manner. (*The worst way*)
- Giving cheerfully, but less than we should give.
- Giving after someone has asked us.
- Giving before we have been asked.
- Giving when we don't know the recipient, but the recipient knows us.
- Giving when we know the recipient, but the recipient doesn't know us.
- Giving when neither party knows the identity of the other.
- Giving to enable the recipient to achieve self-reliance. (*The best way*)

In a materialistic society, where money is king and everyone is selling something to us all the time, we appear terrified of Jesus. Is he really against our dream of pulling ourselves up in society by dint of hard work in order to enjoy a more comfortable life? If we make money, do we have to give all of it away to the poor?

Our fear of Jesus is very real because an aggressively commercial community surrounds us. Everything is for sale! We judge things by their price. Someone wandering around the majestic Chartres Cathedral in France recently had just one question to ask the guide about the ancient architectural treasure: how much did it cost to build? What we don't to see what Jesus meant when he said, "It is very difficult for the wealthy to become part of the Kingdom" (saying 19). We think of the word "difficult" as the opt-out clause. True, Jesus, who believed in the supremacy and transforming power of love, did not say "impossible," but if we are thinking of a way out of the problem of wealth and the Good Society, we should take a good hard look at our own motivation.

In the old days, parents took their children to sports practice for good exercise and an opportunity for the youngsters to have fun and grow their social skills in a competitive environment. Now, many parents' not-so-secret hope is that their baby will grow up to be an outrageously over-paid sports professional. To these sadly misguided parents the social skills of kids working amicably with other kids in the games they play now seem unimportant. Instead they think their babies need to develop, as one crazed father said, "the right killer instinct!" Likewise, at the Olympic Games, going for the gold medal now seems essential for athletes who have been seduced by the media's only-the-gold-will-do attitude. They are mortified to come away with a silver medal or a bronze. Whatever happened to the glory of simply taking part in the world's premier athletic event?

Caring and Sharing

The Good Society requires lots of sharing, and fairness has often been seen as best achieved through the leveling of wealth imbalances in society by taxation. Throughout history, taxes have been a most reviled social instrument. Most people hate them, even though they pay for the essential services we all take for granted that the state will provide. Jesus recognized that we must be prepared to accept some measure of control over our lives by the larger society of which we are a part: "Pay Caesar what belongs to Caesar, and pay God what belongs to God" (saying 24). Taxes may never be popular, but our assessment of them changes in part if we look first at what they are designed to do for the good of all, and only second at what they will do to our pocket. It may even be true that those who make the largest protest against taxation are demonstrating how much the love of money is central to their lives.

Our society sets itself up as providing "caring services" on our behalf. All too often, however, mainly because of bureaucracies, care does not materialize anything like as well as advertised. This can be a lesson for us, opening up our minds to Jesus' basic position. The world is full of sick people, the forgotten elderly, desperate single mothers and their hungry children, and many more. Especially, it is full of socially inadequate and troubled people who are so often found wandering city streets in search of understanding and relief. And if all that is just in the affluent western society, how much more pressing is the world's need outside the richest nations.

It is a brutal world we live in, where young girls are sold into sexual slavery and little children are robbed of their childhood and their future by being forced to work in clothing and carpet-making factories and the like. Is it not very strange that we are quite scared of Jesus when it comes to our being ready to undertake the tasks of caring for others? Does he actually require us to do all those caring jobs personally? Heaven forbid! We don't like to get our hands dirty, or "waste" valuable time away from our social pursuits, or from the serious business of making money. It is a sad comment on western society that the poor, who themselves need care, demonstrate the highest level of personal involvement in sharing and caring for others.

Openness

Let us look again at the process of bringing in the Good Society. Jesus does not talk in a vacuum. He is direct and personal. First he recognizes that we may not want to help, but we must stretch ourselves to do it. "If you only love those who love you, what's special in that? After all, even sinners love people who love them" (saying 38). Caring starts with an understanding of how the world works: "Your heavenly Father makes the sun rise on bad people and good people, and sends rain on the just and the unjust" (saying 37). It seems to be tough out there by design. Are we called to be tough? Jesus believes that costly openness and costly generosity toward others is a cause for happiness: "Be happy, you who go hungry so that the stomach of someone in need may be filled!" (saying 42), and "Love your enemies" (saying 47).

The man in the story who was mugged on the road from Jerusalem to Jericho was in a real mess. One can imagine blood all over the place, but that didn't stop the Samaritan from coming to his aid in a one-on-one rescue encounter, motivated by compassion to clean up the blood and take the victim to a safe, good place where he might recover (saying 44). The foreigner stepped outside of his circle of family and friends to bring the Good Society to his needy neighbor—a thing the priest and the scholar in the story were not prepared to do.

The owner of the vineyard faced opposition from some of his workers when he paid all of them the living wage they all needed (saying 45). He was a man who truly cared for other people, and his story shows how those in authority can work for the Good Society.

Wherever the Good Society is based in the intimate human circles of family, friends, neighborhood, village, town, it has two potential strengths. First, we don't have to tough it out alone, but can have our caring group come in support of our efforts, and help if our resolution or our talents fall short. Second, our group can be inspirational for us to do what we can on our own. We can be filled with compassion: the sprit of openness and caring. The group dynamic can motivate quite shy people to take a lead in doing necessary jobs of rescue and care. Some of us may even find ourselves outside our little circle of friends, acting like the Samaritan by giving aid to total strangers.

Forgiveness

There is another element in the call to be open and caring toward other people. "Forgive our debts as we have forgiven our debtors" (saying 1). This isn't about specific of person-to-person forgiveness; it is about the whole of our attitude and our dealings with other people. "Forgive and you will be forgiven" (saying 46). In the Good Society everyone must generate goodness. If everyone has a forgiving attitude, the balance of forgiveness in society will be sound, and if everybody is caring and open, the balance will be wholesome.

It is absolutely vital that we see this process belonging to every unit of society. As soon as we launch out into the wider society, with all its problems, we can feel overwhelmed. Many people are indifferent, even hostile; so we must remember Jesus' instruction to "Love your enemies" (saying 47) as a basic tenet of our behavior. However hard it is out in the world, in our tenants' association, in a group of friends meeting after work, or whatever group we belong to, forgiveness and mutual help are always possible. Even in the smallest group forgiveness will rarely be easy, but its intimacy heightens the chances of success as we seek together to give and to receive forgiveness.

Starting to train for the marathon is like that. A twenty-six mile run—forget it! But a jog round the block is a start. Marathon runners know a thing or two about the Good Society. They know that you can only do what your body can stand and little more. Then, as you exercise and train, your body offers more opportunities for success. The five-mile run that made you breathless doesn't give you so much trouble; now you can make it to ten miles before becoming winded.

It is the same with forgiveness and openness toward other people and being caring of others in need. You can start working with a group of five or six people; then, not you alone but the whole group can take on another situation, and then another. Look at the life of Mother Teresa. She started in a small way, alone, not able to do much, but intent on comforting Calcutta's dying poor and letting them know that they were loved. Soon, she attracted a company of like-minded women and, with permission from the Vatican, formed a religious order dedicated to the work she had begun. In time, The Missionaries of Charity grew and spread throughout the world.

Each of Mother Teresa's nuns was as committed as she was in drawing the dying into the order's circle of care, but as leader she became extra special to the world. In any community there will be a leader. In the local tenants' association you might be just a member of the team, but you could draw on that experience in your bridge club to lead others into developing a small caring community. This process is like a chain: you are a single loop connected to your friends, each of whom is in other friendship loops, and they extend the chain to their friends, their friends' loops, and so on.

Patience

If we try to picture the Good Society, we may be misled into thinking that the world will change overnight. That was not Jesus' thought. He pictured farmers sowing seed but having a long wait while it germinated, sprouted, grew, and finally ripened (saying 7). The Good Society takes a long time to mature, but if we sow the seed we can expect it will come to harvest. The modern world demands instant results. We ask why people in third-world countries are allowed to die in large numbers from various diseases, or why ethnic wars escalate into genocide, or why innocents perish in terrorist attacks. We want everything solved NOW! But life is not like that; we have to build a helping society that's well organized to provide permanent solutions to hard problems. Of course politicians are appointed to use public funds on our behalf, but in a host of situations, that technique doesn't work at all well. Charities dishing out food today must dish out food tomorrow and the next day and the next. That is part of the hunger solution, but it can't be the whole solution. Unless we all want to work on the hunger problem by sharing our talents and wealth with the poor, it won't ever be solved. That's history. Society fails time and time again. The reason is that we have the wrong kind of society: it is organized from the top down, rather than from the bottom up.

Planning for the Good Society

Experiments in Sharing

So, what kind of society will work, and how do we get it? Think first about your family, or the people around you at work. What draws us together to help others? It is a need we can deal with adequately. It could be a joyful one.

Young Mike, the low-paid office junior, is getting married, and we have learned that his fiancée is pregnant. So we club together to buy gifts for the baby and the couple's new home. That buzz of activity and excitement is one of the occasional human things that draw us together. Then our colleague Tami breaks her leg. Some people cover her work assignments and the office chips in to send flowers. Two or three people go to the hospital to check on her progress. That kindness is not much in either instance. It certainly isn't bringing in a new kind of society, but the human scale is right.

Suppose your company adopts a village in Ethiopia, and each section of the company has a family to care for. Then the company's V.P. arranges for employees to join a Peace Corps team and Oxfam volunteers to help them and ensure that the money collected really did the best job possible of helping the villagers with their acute problems. That would be nearer to building a new society. The beneficiaries would not just be the poor people; the whole office society would be helped by the experience. You could add a host of examples, such as volunteering to build poor people new homes. But the illustrations are not good enough. Can you spot the inadequacy?

Most people know that benevolent activity in such an office community is mostly short lived, touches only a minority of lives, and depends on management's approval. It's really too far from our circle of intimate friends and family, and we cannot sustain the effort just by ourselves. In truth, the office giving help in Ethiopia belongs to a later stage in the development of the Good Society. There's nothing wrong with the effort, unless it turns out to be a corporate do-good activity, where we all get tired of contributing, call the venture off, and let the people down who are already the poorest of the poor.

Working in the Small Group

Our having the right attitudes and sharing our passion within our own small groups create the Good Society. Jesus uses the idea of an oil lamp. "No one lights an oil lamp to hide it under a basket. It's put on a lamp stand where everybody can see its light" (saying 19). Our passion for the Good Society is the light. But its little flame doesn't light up the whole world, just a room.

So, how does this little circle of friends operate? Let us suppose that in the room with us we have three close friends: Jill, Joe, and James. We have all have become excited by the idea of the Good Society, and we share ideas of the help we would like to give to our neighbor, a lonely widow called Jasmine. We know she loves seeing people, and we arrange to offer her daily help with some domestic chores. We bring her the groceries each week and spend time with her in conversation. She shares her pictures, memories, and laughter with us, and even bakes chocolate chip cookies for our weekly meeting.

Jill tells her friends Frances and Frank about our group and with them helps to develop another cell. They invite others in and together they think out the details of some other kind of social project they believe they can sustain over the long run. Joe is something of a loner. He does not easily share his enthusiasm with his small circle of friends but, spurred on by new thinking, he re-connects with his elderly father, seeking to close a forgiveness gap that has driven them apart. James, who is a young and idealistic teacher, tries out his ideas on dozens of people. His excitement gets in the way a bit, but he manages to convince a few of them that the ideas are really workable.

So we find that the enthusiasm that we shared with our friends has resulted in:

- Helping them as individuals and strengthening our bond with them;
- Helping an elderly widow;
- Mending a broken family relationship;
- The formation of a new group with similar ambitions;

- The news of this experiment for a Good Society being spread among people our group members know.

This is the process: not a total reorganization of society, not a proletarian revolution, not the great capitalist wealth-dream—just a group effort in the intimate circle of a few friends. As it works well, the Good Society has started to be realized in us and in them through our common relationship. Not all over the world, but as a beginning in our society. Yet, small though it may be, we and they will immediately feel the benefits of our deepened relationships.

Rejection and Failure

But what if the Good Society doesn't come for you? What if your family won't listen to your ideas? What if your perpetual bubbling enthusiasm causes your friends to take themselves and their interests elsewhere? Jesus knew about rejection. One thing the world knows well about him is that he was finally rejected and crucified. He taught his followers about rejection. One of his stories was of a man who invited his friends to a dinner, but the friends had other priorities and would not come (saying 40). So the party-giver threw his home open to the street people instead. Rejection did not mean he could not go ahead with his planned generosity; he just had to try somewhere else.

Rejection is a theme in the story of the man who was collecting rent from tenant farmers. His servants were beaten and sent away, and when the landlord sent his son they killed him (saying 41). Rejection may be more personal. The master who gave his three slaves money to trade with in his absence found his trust rewarded in varying degrees by two of them, who did their best for him. The third slave resented the master-servant relationship and refused to do anything for him (saying 27). Then there was the high official who was forgiven of a colossal debt, but who spurned his king's spirit of generosity by turning on a fellow official who owed him a trifling sum (saying 49).

From outright rejection, we turn to "do-gooders," those people who so often fail in their caring efforts. There are plenty of them about. Like the corn barely growing on thin soil or surrounded by weeds in Jesus' parable (saying 8), they don't last very long. Such people give at Christmas or in response to a special appeal, then forget entirely about the poor recipients whose need stirred their conscience—until the next Christmas. They may feel genuinely pleased that they have done something to help, but if they do not truly *think out* their charity, their help is of little use. Houseplants die if they are not watered regularly, and starving people die if they have to rely on occasional handouts. Often the do-good scene is acted out in a retirement home or by someone's bedside, where the benevolent do-gooder, even a son or daughter, puts in only an occasional appearance. Then…they…drift…away! People dedicated to sharing and caring (as opposed to "do-gooders") stay the course. They water their houseplants regularly, and they tend to the needy in the same way: as the need requires and not as the caregiver's alternative agenda demands.

Commitment

Jesus understood that any enterprise demanding a complete change of life couldn't be easily accepted by anyone. Our commitment to the Good Society will not be shared universally—at least, not for a while. The hardest part is this: we may simply have to leave behind those people who are unconvinced, and try elsewhere. This is the meaning of Jesus' two statements: "Let the dead bury their own dead: you must go out to announce the Kingdom" (saying 16); and, "Any who come to me and do not hold less dear their father and mother, wife, children, brothers, and sisters—even their own lives, cannot be my disciples" (saying 15). This seems impossibly hard until you remember that Jesus is calling for a complete change of lifestyle (in this version of the saying I have substituted "lifestyle" for "life" to make the sense plainer): "Those who try to preserve their lifestyle will lose it, but those who lose the right to a lifestyle of their choice will keep it" (saying 13). This saying is an enigma, but it does the trick. We simply must change, or we will drop out.

The old ways really are not good enough. Jesus' possible saying that we must be "born again" is describing the total change of lifestyle that must accompany our commitment to the Good Society. But not everyone whose brain likes the idea of social reform will achieve a change of heart. "Try your hardest to get through the narrow door. I tell you, many will attempt to do it, but will not be able" (saying 14).

With that gloomy prediction in mind we want to ask if the Good Society can possibly come in our lifetime. Jesus makes it plain that the

Good Society is breaking out all over (even if we can't see that happening) in the lives of those men and women and children who really want it to happen. What we need, and what he supplies, is the blueprint for action and a clear understanding of our goal. The Good Society may not be universal, by far, but it can be very real in our own experience and in our own lifetime.

Jesus and God

Long before the Christian church ever existed, Jesus saw the Good Society coming through people who had an intimate relationship with God. That is implied by his own belief in God as a loving father, "Abba" (saying 1). God possessed the ability to forgive individuals their wrongdoings. God was the architect of a rebuilt society in which he calls us to serve.

Must we accept Jesus' relationship with God for ourselves? For many his example is the best reason to try to have a relationship with their Creator. Others respect him for his trust in God, but in all honesty don't intend to live their lives with that faith. The Good Society clearly includes both types of people in its work.

Jesus talks about the wide variety of people growing up together in the world. In his story of the Pharisee and the Tax Collector (saying 36), he made a strong point that God doesn't accept our self-centered judgments about each other, just because we are devout and morally upright. Jesus does not impose any pre-qualifications on people who commit themselves to the Good Society. The main thing we need to bring is our dire need to transform both our own life and the life of our present society, in accordance with his principles. That's not a qualification based on belief or religious correctness, but on our desire to work humbly and patiently for justice, mercy, forgiveness, and peace in the world.

Visualizing the Changes

We are entering an era in which a large and growing proportion of the world's huge population is secular. Some may want to know God better; some may have tried to find God but have been disappointed in their search; some feel that God, as characterized by the world's religions, is totally unknowable. The fact that, two thousand years ago, Jesus of Nazareth told people where he stood does not bind everyone for all time. But, as has happened with many wise thinkers, Jesus is a teacher whose goals and methods have stood the test of time, whenever invoked, even if they have not been fully implemented. God's plan or not, we still have failed to put Jesus' teachings to the test.

The truth is that we are rather overwhelmed by the enormity of the idea that society can actually change for the better. This feeling is not least because we are so caught up with building a nest egg for ourselves that we imagine we must be living contrary to Jesus' intentions. The heart of this difficulty is our own negativity. We like to project difficulties that don't exist. We persuade ourselves that, since we hesitate to change our lifestyle, others will do the same. But that's just not true! Most people are quite willing to change their lifestyle if they are convinced it is a good thing to do.

First, let us understand that Jesus is a realist. He does not see society transformed in the way the Marxists did, for example. There will be no vast proletarian revolution. The seed grows secretly for a long time; the Good Society breaks out here and there unobtrusively. You don't see it at first, but it is coming. Patience is one of the characteristics of change, as the widow woman understood (saying 30). In the story of the two brothers (saying 50), Jesus does not even finish the tale with a tidy ending because the important issue was how forgiveness in a family was being worked out, and not how long that process was going to take.

Put another way—we are considering a process akin to that of building a fine musical instrument, or writing a major biography. It will take time to transform the world for the better, and that job will not be completed during our lifetime. But human society has already started on the slow process of becoming the Good Society. Our task is to help speed that process, because, even if global reform is not fully realized, we can certainly enjoy the fruits of any changes for the better that affect our own lives and the lives of those around us for whom we have a care.

If it's a slow process creating change in society, how can we find motivation to get involved? Will we ever see real change in our lifetime? The answer given is quite explicit. Jesus envisioned groups of people enjoying the coming-about of the Good Society, just like a farmer sowing seed on different types of soil. Where the soil was good, and where it supported the crop well, "in some areas it had a yield of thirty, in others of sixty, and in others of one hundred times what had been planted there" (saying 8). So the results depend on the soil's fertility, which I take to mean the receptiveness of each little group of people who are aware of the possibility of renewal in their society. The yield in the best soil in that part of the world was nine or ten times the usual harvest, so the hundredfold yield is what people in the stock market call a 1,000% appreciation. The answer is that the Good Society can be our experience, even if it has not arrived for everyone, everywhere.

Hopes and Expectations

Let us examine our hopes for the community of which we are a part and, playing the fairy godmother trick, make three wishes for society. Let's have the traditional *Health, Wealth, and Happiness*:

Health: We certainly wish health for our family and friends, and we see the prevention and cure of every disease, and of malnutrition, as excellent goals. Currently there may be a sick person in our family or circle of friends, and we wish that we could somehow mobilize things to bring healing. We wish for the health of the whole world, as well. This involves ample cheap, preventive medicine; an end to war and the pollution of land, water, and air; the preservation of other species; the restoration of the earth's natural beauty, which we have destroyed; and an end to the grim industrial cities, shantytowns, and ghettoes of the poor. We remember also that good health is both physical and psychological. Mental illness is so often disregarded.

Wealth: For society as a whole this means universal fair distribution of possessions. We want people motivated to make the best of themselves at work, but dislike unbridled greed. That's often as true in families and little groups of people as in the larger world. Wealth also means bringing quality into the things we buy—clothes, furniture, houses, and so on. Getting rid of badly made and badly designed products sold to unsuspecting poor people at unreasonable prices has also to do with wealth. More than anything else it is the need to raise up the poor until their lives are no longer made miserable by the absence of the necessities of life. If possible, the basic luxuries affluent folk take for granted should be available to all.

Happiness: The last of these three wishes also means an end to war and terrorism and mob rule. Happiness implies justice in society, good relationships, openness, and forgiving attitudes. It is the friendliness of people in the street, and the caring attitude shown by the people who direct the life of our society: school teachers, administrators, politicians, and business people. It may be difficult now to imagine true happiness in the wide world, but how about our village, our group of friends, our family? May we not help other people realize their modest dreams?

Consequences

If we name these goals as being among our wildest expectations, then our quest of the Good Society begins. As we work for change, and meet with success, our opportunities will multiply. Remember the three slaves given trading money by their master while he was absent (saying 27)? The two who did their best and made a profit were given new sums with which to go on trading. Even when we fail initially we may be given another chance (saying 39). When everything seems against us, and we must make a desperate attempt to succeed, in the end it can turn out all right (saying 28). So it's not so impossible to believe that the things we know are for the good of society will come about, at least in our little circle, and we will be blessed by that change.

How can we fail to dedicate ourselves to a renewed Good Society that directly benefits our life? Jesus pictures a city on a hill, that cannot be hidden (saying 18). Our ambition to improve things makes other people notice us. It may that our goals are only recognized by a small group; we may be just a little light in the room where a few can see us. Jesus suggests that grasping a worthwhile ambition is a life-changing thing. People sold everything to buy the field with treasure in it; the dealer sold his entire inventory so he could afford the single exquisite pearl (saying 17). We begin to turn a corner when we see the vision Jesus saw. Suddenly we start asking not *whether* but *how* people can get the health, wealth, and happiness they need. Then we start to apply this vision to our relationships and become enablers, sharing the way to fulfillment with others. Finally, as we explain our vision to other people, they pick it up and join the work.

People Who Changed Society

Gautama Siddartha, the Buddha, had a life-changing experience. When he was a rich young man he had a vision of the true nature of life. As he wrestled to come to grips personally with the sickness, decay, and death of other people in society, he himself began to change. He applied the experience to his own life and pondered on what he could do about it. His thinking and teaching attracted other people, becoming a worldwide religious movement helping to correct people's attitudes and change their lives for the better. The Buddha's response was not "Christian" (he lived well before the time of Jesus), but it was true to the vision of a Good Society. Indeed his experience is right on the mark. Westerners may find the language of Buddhism difficult to grasp at first, but the ideas should be examined with care for the insights they bring to bear on the human condition.

From the twelfth century comes an often-quoted example of a man who dedicated himself to living in obedience to the teaching of Jesus. The spendthrift son of a wealthy merchant, he relinquished his affluence, adopting a lifestyle of poverty. Francis of Assisi drew to himself many converts, one of whom was the young heiress Clare of Assisi. They founded two religious orders, one for men and the other for women, asking their members to serve the poor and to embrace poverty, simplicity, and a joyful life in order to follow the teaching and example of Jesus. The Franciscan Order and the Poor Clares are still continuing their work of service in many parts of the world today.

In a different way, Jean-Henri Dunant responded to human need. A Swiss observer of the bloody battle of Solférino between the French and Austrian armies in 1862, Dunant organized emergency relief for the wounded. He saw there was a continuing need to relieve suffering in both war and peacetime, and he proposed that other countries be involved. The humanitarian organization he started has now grown to embrace countries the world over, and not just Christians but Muslims as well, in the International Red Cross and Red Crescent Movement. Dunant also proposed an international agreement concerning the war-wounded, and in 1864 the first Geneva Convention came into being. In

1895 Dunant was awarded the very first Nobel Prize for Peace.

Such vision is not confined to men or to those whose name is universally known. In 1841 a frail young schoolteacher, Dorothea Dix, was asked to begin a Sunday school class in a prison in Massachusetts, USA. There she saw with horror the inhumane treatment of the mentally challenged and mentally ill. Depending on her own resources, Dix began a campaign to improve conditions for these hapless inmates. She traveled throughout her own state, investigating its prisons, and subsequently convinced the legislators there to improve the patients' conditions with brand-new facilities. Then she took her campaign further, convincing legislators in fifteen American states to build new facilities to house the mentally ill. Thirty-two such hospitals resulted from her efforts. She carried her campaign abroad, notably in Italy where she persuaded the Pope to inspect the grim prison facilities in Rome. Unlike the Buddha and Dunant, Dorothea Dix did not found a reform movement, but her legacy has been a change in public attitudes and welfare provisions for mentally ill people throughout the world.

These people all turned a corner in their thinking—and helped our human society to turn a corner as well. Indeed, they qualify as having been *born again*, not in the church's understanding of expressing belief in Christ, but in their having entered a new phase in their thinking and living. Each experienced a permanent change, which brought profound personal satisfaction to their lives. The problem for many of us with the stories of such people as the Buddha, Francis and Clare, Dunant, and Dix, is that we have real difficulty in believing that we can copy their lead! We feel so inadequate in comparison with them. Yet we can influence others in a way that is quite remarkable, if we will only try.

A good example of the human "chain" working for the Good Society began in 1832 when Samuel Gridley Howe opened a small school in Boston for blind children. One of them, Laura Bridgeman, was not only blind, but also deaf and mute. Using tactile signing, he managed to convey to Laura the possibility of learning through touch. One of Howe's pupils, Johanna (Annie) Sullivan, was nearly blind until a successful operation restored some of her sight. Her experience of the school and her reading of Howe's pioneering work with Laura led Annie to apply for the job of tutor to a difficult young girl, Helen

Keller. Like Laura, Helen was blind, deaf, and mute, but Annie was able to train her by means of the manual alphabet and with Braille. Helen Keller became internationally known for the way she overcame her severe handicaps, for her academic success, and her promotion of good work among the blind.

Can we be like the dim-sighted Annie? Still too challenging? Even if we retreat psychologically from the possibility of ever achieving something significant ourselves, we can always console ourselves by being part of a team that nurtures and encourages bright achievers to do great things. Every great reformer, every successful leader had family members, teachers, and friends whose influence launched them on their career. At the heart of the Good Society is not greatness of achievement but consistency of purpose. The Good Society is fueled by the lives of those who strive to be true to their vision. "Grapes are not picked from thorn bushes, nor figs from thistles" (saying 32). Jesus looks for honesty and integrity in the people who make up the Good Society, not for specific achievement. He looks for the modesty with which we may recognize our failings when dealing with the failings of others (saying 35). He looks also for us to maintain high standards of self discipline: "What goes into your mouth will not make you unclean; what comes out of your mouth makes you dirty" (saying 34).

Yogesh K. Gandhi tells of a woman in India who, with her son, walked 300 miles on foot to try to get Mahatma Gandhi to help her change her son's poor eating habits. She asked the Mahatma to persuade him not to eat sugar. Gandhi turned her away, requesting that she bring her boy back in two weeks. Disappointed, she did what she was asked, and on her return the Mahatma talked with the boy and successfully persuaded him to drop the sugar habit. At this the mother asked Gandhi to explain why he would not talk to the boy two weeks before. He replied, "Two weeks ago, *I* was eating sugar."

Small Beginnings

The vision of the Good Society can truly attract us, and when we have overcome our personal feelings of inadequacy, we can commit our lives to it. We should not doubt that social change is already under way. What we must do is to ensure that this new way of living becomes the hallmark of our own circle of family and friends. We must see that our personal circle is one link of a continuous chain. People who know us have their own friendship links as well. As our relationship shines in their lives, so they have opportunities to pass the experience on. Jesus sees this process in terms of the tiny mustard seed. "The mustard seed, which is the smallest of all seeds, is planted. It grows into a large plant and becomes a shelter for the birds" (saying 4). He also sees this in terms of the outreach we can make toward others who have lost their direction in life. When a sheep wandered off, the shepherd took action. He left the ninety-nine on the pasture and went to look for the lost one until he found it (saying 5). From our circle of friends one or more may be dispatched to help someone in need.

Jesus taught that children have a special part to play in the Good Society. In her book *Learning the Skills of Peacemaking* (Appendix II), schoolteacher Naomi Drew tells how by learning in class alternative ways to handle personal relationships with simple peace-making skills, children's attitudes toward their peers have been transformed. Naomi told me that some of her children's parents have also learned from them peacemaking techniques that have benefited their marriages and other relationships. "The Kingdom belongs to childlike people" (saying 2). By their innocent examples, children are able to teach us the humility and trustfulness that are hallmarks of the Good Society. When we realize that, our hesitation about our own involvement should take flight. If a child can unself-consciously promote the Good Society, so can we!

Running The Marathon Of Life

The Runner's Goals

My high-school class was made to take part in cross-country running. The race itself was nothing like the 26-mile marathon. It was only three or four miles long but involved us in plodding through muddy fields, wrestling with ancient gates, dodging under dripping trees, and, when we finally got back to school, being physically beaten by the teacher for taking too much time. In consequence of these difficulties, my goal became escaping from the dreaded exercise. Armed with a strong note from my sympathetic mother, I negotiated a less-demanding routine of exercises in the gymnasium.

The marathon runner has two main goals. The first is to do better than before. The second is to win each race. Most dedicated runners say that improving on their personal performance is an all-important goal. Winning the race is a combination of being in the peak of performance and having opponents that can be beaten. Nobody wins a marathon without serious, long-term training.

People who are committed to running the marathon of life also have two goals. The first is identical to that of the runner: finding ways to improve on their past performance. The second is bringing experience of the Good Society to the circles of people in which they belong. Winning isn't an equivalent, but achieving any lasting enlargement of the Good Society is very like a victory, however small it may be. This may feel like a very restricted objective for those who wish to magic the Good Society into every corner of the globe! But just as the Olympic marathon, though the most-watched race in the world, is only one of many such races involving far more people, so also the Good Society circles to which you or I belong may be only a tiny part of the activity of the whole reformed human community.

The idea of a truly universal Good Society, embracing all people of all races and types, must be our goal. That is rather like the hope many athletes have that everyone will come to share in the benefits of their vigorous exercise. But in real terms such universal outreach can only be a consequence of thousands of small but growing Good

Societies. That is because it is best expressed through my relationship with you; yours with Xavier; his with Anna; and so on. The roots of grass make up a lawn, but they only live in relation to the roots next to them. If we don't understand by now that Jesus was aiming to develop a grass-roots movement, we get him wholly wrong.

Impatience

The failure of many attempts to create a better society may have resulted from people's impatience to see the end results before starting the process properly. I suspect, for example, that the horrors of the Spanish Inquisition, where Christian clergy investigated, condemned, and executed large numbers of fine, faithful people for breaches of conformity to the church's doctrines, probably began with declarations of the very highest of motives. The priests wanted to ensure that their society remained true to God, expressing their highest ideals. But they got so absorbed by their narrow thinking that they failed to grasp the essence of Jesus' teaching. The more zealous their enforcement, the more warped and brutalized their lives, until they became the very opposite of the one for whom they professed veneration—Christ. Unfortunately this was not the only time such unutterable violence in the name of God happened in the Christian church's history. Many attempts have been made to mold society through brute force rather than by love and the slow, patient way of forgiveness.

Community of Heart and Mind

The vision of the Good Society is of tolerance of other people's differences; being understanding, open, and helpful towards them; sharing time and resources to help them achieve their potential; and offering them forgiveness in the face of their mistakes. This must be a shared experience, in which not just one group or individual takes the initiative, but all of us are deeply involved, in accordance with our abilities, and allowing for people's psychological scarring and frailties.

This kind of relating-in-community leads to happiness and positive life experiences for everybody involved. All will benefit by receiving greater acceptance from other people, a deeper experience of their forgiveness, and a greater common concern that they will be successful. The goal of the Good Society includes the warm, good feeling we have experienced in our own personal circles in their best moments. We see it also expressed in our intention to make larger reforms stick, and the renewed society growing stronger and more fair.

Deep in our response to Jesus' teaching is the feeling that all people possess inner loneliness and isolation to some degree. Yet there have also been times in life when we reached out from our isolation toward other people and found them doing the same thing. Such moments of deepened friendship have brought out the best in us and the best in them. For some people this experience has been repeated often; for others it is treasured but has happened infrequently. For all of us, the experience of reaching out, accepting, and being accepted is a deep delight. It gives us the warm glow of personal wholeness.

Such good feelings cannot be bought. They can only be encouraged and worked for by our patient persistence and truthful adherence to the way of right mindfulness and right relationships. Nor are they confined to a single friendship. That's too easy, and too low a goal. For our sense of self-worth to be truly complete, we have an enormous inner need for good relationships with everyone around us. Of course, we cannot control the way others feel about life, and what they will bring to any encounter with us. We can at least be true to our vision of what our relationship toward them should be like. More than that, we can bring the strength that experience of the Good Society in our circle gives to all our encounters and relation-building attempts.

Thinking about this, I am reminded that, for the majority of people, the family is their primary place for wonderful, supporting experiences. Sadly this is not true for those who must look elsewhere for what we call "family love." Our first taste of self-worth is so often at the loving hands of a parent, an older friend, a sibling, or a teacher. I recall swelling with pride when praised by my father for solving a little mechanical problem that had baffled him. Decades later I can still feel the warm glow his approval gave me.

For some people their high point in life was a friendship in college, in the military, or on their first job. But just as miserable children in poor Romanian orphanages have sickened and even died for lack of affection, so we can grow up really stunted emotionally if an experience of self-worth has rarely been given to us. There are some unfortunate people who cannot point to a single meaningful and supportive relationship in their lives. They are among those for whom the Good Society must be created and sustained, the lost sheep for whose rescue and consolation we must go in search.

The Bountiful Harvest

In his parables of the man scattering seed that grew in places to yield an enormous crop (saying 8), and of the tiny mustard seed growing into a large bush (saying 4), Jesus indicated his conviction that we are going to be astonished by the bountiful growth of the Good Society. That's because it does not come only from the activity of men and women, but also from divine impulse and divine benevolence. What does the amazing harvest represent? Is it the work done by the human being who sowed the seed, or is it the fruitfulness of the ground? There is no doubt that the hand of God is in the maturing of the seed, yet we are called to be involved in the good work of sowing it, so we truly have a part to play, and satisfaction to enjoy at the end.

Our life today may mean less now than when we make an appraisal of it in our old age. Picture yourself sitting in that proverbial rocking chair, remembering and pondering your past. Your prudence may have left you comfortably endowed for your old age and, providing your wealth has not become a barrier to relationships, you may be truly satisfied that you have played your part in encouraging other people in a practical way. Some will look back upon their exercise of power or their enjoyment of fame. If, as a politician, a leader in industry, a noted thinker or teacher, a renowned artist or writer, you have wielded influence and power in the lives of other people, you must ask yourself if you overcame the dangers associated with your position. Were you readily available to others? Were you willing to be a servant in society as well as a leader? Undoubtedly, those leaders who retain the "human touch" can be part of the Good Society.

Jesus spoke about barriers to our becoming successfully integrated in the Good Society. We remember the magistrate who had no fear of God and did not care about other people (saying 30). He only gave way to the widow because he wanted to get rid of her. Then there was the Pharisee who was convinced that he was the best thing God had made since unleavened bread! He thought no one could match his piety, goodness, and generosity (saying 36). Then there was the stupid official in royal service who would not forgive a trifling debt after he had been released from a colossal debt of his own making (saying 49). People like these cut themselves off from society by their insensitivity and anger. Perhaps you know one or two people like that. Having thought of them, turn the spotlight on yourself: If you only love those people who love you, what's so special? "After all, sinners love people who love them" (saying 38). It may be hard to be self-critical, but neglecting to make a healthy self-evaluation is the hallmark of social disease and death. That's true for society as a whole (e.g., racism and other forms of discrimination) as much as for individuals in society.

Team Building

Marathon runners may seem solitary types, but many of them belong to running clubs. It helps runners' morale to be able to join others in trials and races, pitting themselves against other people whose worth can be measured. There's a sense of cooperation in a running club that gives strength to the individual, especially when things are not going too well. After all, the inner game of running is not so much about breasting the tape first in an occasional race (though that really helps) as trying time after time to improve on your past performance.

It is difficult, not knowing your personal circumstances, for me to translate this experience into your own team building for the Good Society. Interpret my words, if you can, as I make the following suggestions:

First, we must create our own agenda. Our interests and experiences are unique. For some of us the thought of involving people to improve the life of our local community, or preserve the environment of the wetlands near our home, or care for a poor family is the first idea that comes into our head. The inspiration is already within us; next must come the gathering of people to do the job. For others the very idea of taking an initiative and leading anyone is more than we can imagine. We want to be a support person, one who will give encouragement and take on some of the shared tasks. Both leading and being led are important to us; the only thing that is not an option is doing nothing at all.

Next, whether leader or follower, we are all involved in the rebuilding of our society. That means we must express ourselves to other people. If they don't know what we mean by the Good Society we must try to explain. Here's where the team can come in. You know the pattern already: your best friend is the person you want to help understand what is in your heart. You want him or her to be part of a circle working for the betterment of society. (You could lend this book, but though it might help with the explanations, it cannot be enough, because living relationships, not books, are the heart of the Good Society.)

Then, having won the acceptance of one friend, you start on another who is invited to coffee and meets the two of you. This way you build a little circle of friends. The conversation comes round to your common interest, and you suggest to your latest friend that he or she will be very welcome at a meeting of your group. You are not asking for anything, like money or service, just that you want at this point to deepen your friendships, look for common goals, share experiences, and tackle common problems.

Invitations may fail but true friendships do not. We can always tell our family and friends what we are up to! The runner comes back and tells Dad that it was a good day out on the track. We can tell our friend that it was interesting visiting the family on 14th Street and getting to know how difficult things had been for them.

Remember, we need to be both patient and persistent. "Ask – and it will be given to you. Seek – and you will find. Knock – and it will be opened for you" (saying 29). The neighbor who woke up his friend in the middle of the night was rebuffed initially. But Jesus sees persistence paying off: "Let me tell you, even though he won't get up out of friendship to give you anything, he'll certainly get up and give whatever is needed because you were not ashamed to ask" (saying 31). Making the world a better place is a cause for which we need not be ashamed to ask people to give their help. Indeed, it is the ring of conviction in our voice that stirs good people into action. We have to be that light shining in the darkness, because being a blob in the darkness won't get us anywhere.

As we work on our marathon of life other people will join us. It takes time—indeed it *must* take time if we are doing the job properly. Not only should we become fully aware of the nature of our relationship with other people, but also we have to be open, discussing social issues with them to avoid lapsing into introversion. There must be a dynamic element in our common experience, which is why our group needs a project to bring the bounty of the Good Society to others who might never have the experience. Here's an example:

Sue and Nikki were high school best friends. Shortly after leaving school they broke up over a boy, with hard feelings expressed on both sides, and did not meet again for many years. One day Sue discovered they were living in the same part of another town. (The boy had disappeared from the scene a long time ago.) She explained the idea of the Good Society to Nikki, and after some soul-searching, tears, and cups of coffee, their friendship was re-established.

Then came the dynamic part. In Nikki's apartment block was Lucy, a single mother with two little children. She was barely able to cope, scraping by on the minimum wage. Her son was running wild and the little girl was always sickly. The mother was, not surprisingly, suffering from depression. So the two friends found ways to help. Nikki formed a helping relationship with Lucy. Sue, now a high school teacher, began tutoring the boy with his reading and numbers. Her husband, Bob, was drawn in to "big brother" the boy on Saturdays, taking him to Little League where he learned to channel some of his energy. Nikki's husband, Raoul, a chef, was roped into the group and was able to design some inexpensive meals that helped the little girl get the nourishment she needed to grow strong and healthy.

Although this is an imaginary account of the process, the reality is there. Sue's initiative brought her into relationship with Nikki again and helped them both to commit to a good cause and to share their ideas with other people. What started as a twosome ended with seven people becoming involved. We might imagine that in their other social circles, Sue, Nikki, Bob, Raoul, and Lucy might soon begin to stimulate similar responses. The progress in Lucy's children would benefit other children and their teachers as well. What a harvest!

Team Dynamics

Every team has its own dynamic. Indeed, one of the problems can be that team excitement leads to unwise ambition. The desire to develop a group with our message and our methods can lead to problems of personal ambition, and to groups growing and growing in size until they come to resemble small organizations. Neither personal dominance nor large size is a healthy element.

Some psychologists have suggested that we find it difficult to have close personal relationships in a group with more than 8-12 people. Our little circles must be just that—*little* circles—otherwise we will not enjoy the depth of relationship needed to make the enterprise a success. Openness, care, forgiveness, support—these are all elements that demand time and patience. Should the group get too big, people will be left out on the edge of the circle and we will have failed.

Some people will always remain subjects for our caring. Old Arthur, who is very deaf and crippled, may not even fully understand the motivation for our helping him. That's all right, because we have brought him some of the fruits of the Good Society in his declining years. It is what we would hope for ourselves. We must try to do for others what we would have them do for us, and we must be prepared also to receive from others the same. In his children's story *The Water Babies*, Charles Kingsley named two ladies: "Mrs. Do-As-You-Would-Be-Done-By," and "Mrs. Be-Done-By-As-You-Did." This sums it up.

From the isolation of trying to initiate a microcosm of the Good Society around us, we may eventually find ourselves in more than one team working for social renewal. Jesus seems to have experimented both with a small group of students and, on one occasion, a larger number of seventy disciples who were sent out with his message. But the twelve disciples were his core group. I see the position of the teacher and his students as being a little different from our group of equals. Jesus had the task of enunciating the message; ours is the task of putting it into practice.

So how far must our team go? There's a constant temptation for groups to grow bigger and bigger, so there is the risk that more and more practical work will be taken on until the pace kills the enthusiasm of members. The size issue should be fairly simple: I see a norm of six or eight people becoming involved in any one group, reaching out to a few other individuals in care. Above that size one or two members of the group should split off so that a second group can be formed.

It is better to have two or three people doing a thorough job of relating to each other and helping in the caring work of the world, than to have a large group fail because it falls apart, or becomes stressed by an unreasonable amount of activity. This leads to half-committed people becoming "do-gooders" and losing the impetus to reform their tiny corner of the world. Building the Good Society is done by living naturally and thoughtfully, not by frenetic striving to prove how good we are, and trying to drag society along by the heel

Will it work? You will never know unless you try it for yourself.

Getting Ready To Run

If you are going to run a marathon you must buy a pair of running shoes, light clothes, and a water bottle before setting off down the road. (Pity the poor man who ran naked and shoeless with news of the battle of Marathon that first time!) You have to leave the warm fire, the coffee pot, and the easy chair behind. Never mind how far you are planning to run today—it's the tying on of the shoes, the closing of the door behind you, and that first, stiff trot as your muscles begin to warm up that count. People may know what you are planning to do. Some will tell you that they are not cut out for such a strenuous activity. Others of your family and friends may come along from time to time.

The marathon of life will be a similar experience. You have to take the initiative yourself. Others may join you, or you may be invited into an existing group, which makes things easier. As this marathon is always about the quality of relationships you build and your creativity in bringing good to others, you will always be "on your mettle" and a little on your own in taking initiatives.

There are plenty of people who tell reformers that the world cannot be changed. You must stay focused on the idea that you are not out to change the whole world but to improve one little corner of it. Even when you tell them, some folks won't be impressed. That may be because they don't really want to change their own lives and fear the consequences of doing so. It's especially true for people closest to you, who think they understand you best. For them "the proof of the pudding is in the eating." If you change and lead them they may follow, though Jesus said that was not always going to happen (sayings 13-18).

The best you can do is to encourage your nearest and dearest to maintain the best relationships with you; that really is possible. Then set about doing your bit for others beyond the family so that your own folk can see what you mean by an open, caring, and forgiving attitude, and maintain your standards over the long term lest you drop from your commitment (saying 33). The common sense of this method is that we will see each group or circle prove that even a small city on a hill cannot be hidden. It's the "vision thing"! Some people just have to see results before they will commit themselves to anything. That's part of their inner need. They know that "grapes are not picked from thorn bushes, nor figs from thistles" (saying 32). So you must simply do your personal best as a pioneer in the work of reform.

Attempting to do your personal best means examining your whole being. Not just your physical preparation, healthy diet, adequate sleep, exercise, and so on, but also your mental and emotional life and your relationships. These are the qualities that lead to clear goals, patience with yourself, tolerance for other people, and, above all, maintaining the faith that you can do a good job.

In the marathon of life we should take the sayings of Jesus to heart and apply them to ourselves. Choose practical ones to begin with, like those about the act of giving we discussed earlier. Giving is not just money; it is more often that we give time to support other people, and pay attention to their needs. Spending a few hours every Wednesday night giving food to the homeless, sticking stamps on envelopes for a charity's mailing effort, visiting an elderly relative or neighbor on a regular basis: all such self-giving takes time. We can be destitute but still have personal time to give. The gift of time can be a real gift.

Our skills can also be put to good use. I know you can read (even if you skip a bit), so why not share that gift with a child who has failed to develop reading skills adequately? Your facility with mathematical problems can help people struggling with debts, and so on. If our help is the philanthropic gift of money, we must stand guard against failure through self-centeredness (saying 21). The issue of giving money is one in which we must use savvy, while remaining "as innocent as a dove." The innocence is our purpose in helping others; the shrewdness is in knowing how best to do it. If we must confront those in authority, being "as sly as a snake" will be demonstrated in our persistence and being "as innocent as a dove" in the rightness of our cause (saying 25).

While working in a global volunteer organization, I learned that when feeding the hungry there is no point in doing without any food yourself, or you will have no strength to do your work. Those workers who starved themselves in sympathy with the poor around them were sent home as useless. It may well be a form of self-denial to do that.

But if the job is to help build people's strength, it really demands we also maintain our health and strength, and our economic stability.

So you can start down the road of life. Just like a runner you can monitor how you are doing month by month, using a journal, perhaps. You may leave the others behind if they won't come, but you may not criticize them for lagging behind. It's your job to lead, so buy your mental running shoes today and start running.

The Finish Line

Jesus' confidence in the present reality and the eventual success of the Good Society is quite infectious. It will require dedication, even sacrifice, on our part, but the result is unsurpassed! I suspect that he was no less impatient than we are to see society reformed. What a daunting task to suggest the principles of social reform in the face of religious hostility and incomprehension! But Jesus looked with a loving eye on the poor, the sick, and the disregarded members of his own community. He knew the meaning of oppression, war, and merciless brutality in an age that was certainly no less brutal than our own. Maybe he thought genuine social change could come sooner than it has done; certainly many of his immediate followers believed it would. I suspect he fired their enthusiasm with the imperative of completing the changes in society within their own brief lifetime.

Our confidence in this generation is based on the enduring quality of Jesus' principles and goals. He expected a period of organic change for the better would be necessary. We should acknowledge that it is already in progress. There's an awfully long way to go before the Good Society is fully realized, but the world is somewhat more kind and understanding now than in former times, even if greed and hatred often seem to rule our lives. Many people are truly grappling with the inequality of women in society, with the curse of racism, with the tragic exploitation of children and the poor, with our exploitation of the earth and with other barriers to human understanding and fairness.

We should want to see the process continuing and to believe that it can be speeded by our involvement. Once we have grasped that possibility, we have received the good news of social salvation. As we make a true commitment to the regeneration of society as the cause for lifelong personal action, we will discover a moment of enlightenment as we are "born again" into the community of the Good Society.

For many people Jesus' teaching about God will readily be accepted. It is a comforting idea that the ultimate concern of the Divine Creator is to see the welfare of all people. Jesus talked of tiny sparrows being within the knowledge of God, and therefore we human beings must concern God even more (saying 11). He also spoke of our needing to trust God, whose loving-kindness is always directed for our ultimate good, whatever our response (saying 12). Whether or not we accept Jesus' belief in "Abba," his divine loving parent, the Father who feeds, forgives, and shelters us, we should accept his concept as pointing us toward the essential reliability of the cosmic order of life.

We can accept the idea of the Good Society either because it is God's or because it is in accordance with the unifying principles of life. Hatred, greed, and social injustice are part of the atrophy that tears society asunder; love, sharing, and social justice create the opposite cosmic force, drawing society together and healing its wounds.

Commitment to the Good Society boils down to a basic trust of life. That is not easy for those who have lost the trust they had as children, but it still can be found deep within. Just as we must hope that polluted air will still fill our lungs with enough life-giving oxygen, and trust that the adulterated food will give us strength for the day ahead, so we can take one more step. We must build on whatever level of trust we still possess to accept that life is essentially good.

Jesus gave clues as to how life should be lived. Hundreds of wise teachers and thousands of dedicated lives fill in the gaps and expand our vision of the Good Society. But in the end we must break away from the pack and create, in our own life and in the lives of the people we know, a miniature Good Society. Then we will have played our part and will have the satisfaction of doing so, and our society may have come a bit closer to its divinely ordained goal. Yet in the race of life, unlike the marathon race, we will discover that no one ever needs to beat anyone to the tape, because by simply taking part together in the race that is set before us, amazingly we all become winners.

A Check List for Activists

Here is a handy reference list of the main points Jesus made. Basically following the order of this book, it pinpoints issues we may want to raise and gives the references to the primary Bible verses and the page number in the book for each of Jesus' sayings and the main commentary. You can use the first appendix for further detailed explanations and the other Bible verses.

Serious students of the teaching of Jesus need to have a good understanding of his sayings, which hang together and provide us with a very clear plan for action. You may wish to become familiar with the way in which Jesus deals with the nature of the Good Society and its supporters' essential attitudes, so that you may understand his answers with greater accuracy. It is surprisingly easy to get into a fog as to what exactly Jesus said about this or that. The table below will help you to sort things out. You may also wish to commit to memory whatever you regard as his most important teachings—or you could learn all fifty sayings as a valuable practical exercise of commitment and devotion to his way of life.

Some of the references are to the newly discovered Gospel of Thomas. Because it is a very early reference to Jesus' teaching, it has great authority. If you want to stick to the four canonical gospels, Matthew, Mark, Luke, and John, that's fine as well. It is good to remember that many people wrote accounts of Jesus, some of whom remembered fairly accurately what he had said, while others simply recorded their best memory of him—after 40 years or more. The quotations given in this book are those regarded by the distinguished scholars of the Jesus Seminar as their best estimate of the sayings that were most accurately remembered.

Training for the Marathon of Life

A Check List of Jesus' Sayings

Our Issues	The Sayings	Bible Verse
Who is in charge of the Good Society?	* Father, may your name be sacred. May your Kingdom come.	Luke 11:2b-4
What is the Good Society like?	* A Woman who took yeast and kneaded 50 lbs of dough.	Matthew 13:33
	* A tiny mustard seed growing into a large plant.	Thomas 20:2-3
	* A shepherd with 100 sheep who went off to rescue a lost one.	Thomas 107:1-3
When will the Good Society come?	* It is spreading across the world and people don't realize it is there.	Thomas 113:2-4
	* It is like a seed growing secretly in the ground.	Mark 4:26-29
What will God provide for us in the Good Society?	* Give us each day our daily bread. Forgive our debts. Preserve us from temptation.	Luke 11:2b-4
	* God will reward our efforts with incredible bounty.	Mark 4:3-8
	* God will give good things to those who ask for them.	Matthew 7:9-11
Who will benefit from the Good Society?	* The poor, the hungry, those who are crying, will be happy.	Luke 6:20b-21
	* Don't be fearful: you are worth more than a flock of birds.	Matthew 10:29-31
	* Won't he care for you, though you trust him so little?	Matthew 6:25-30
How can we take part in the Good Society?	* The Kingdom belongs to childlike people.	Mark 10:14b
	* Those who lose their right to life will keep it.	Luke 17:33
	* Try your hardest to get through the narrow door.	Luke 13:24
	* Be prepared to sacrifice everything.	Luke 14:26
	* Leave the old life behind.	Luke 9:60b
	* Give everything for this treasure.	Matthew 13:44-46
	* Be visible like a bright light.	Mark 4:21b
Is it possible to be wealthy and powerful and be a part of the Good Society?	* It's very difficult for the wealthy to become part of the Kingdom.	Matthew 19:23b-24
	* Invest in other people.	
	* Give secretly to charity.	Thomas 95:1-2
	* You cannot serve both God and wealth	Matthew 6:3

	at the same time. * The rich man's story. * Pay Caesar what belongs to Caesar, and pay God what belongs to God.	Matthew 6:24 Thomas 6:1-2 Matthew 12:17
Qualities	**What qualities should we possess to belong to the Good Society?**	
1. Shrewdness	* Be sly as a snake and innocent as a dove. * Think out your problems rationally. * Be productive people. * Be shrewd in business.	Matthew 10:16b Luke 12:58-59 Matthew 25:14-28 Luke 16:1-8a
2. Persistent patience	* Ask – Seek – Knock. * The widow's tale. * Borrowing bread.	Matthew 7:7-8 Luke 18:2-5 Luke 11:5-8
3. Honesty and Integrity	* Grapes and thorns. * When salt loses its flavor. * What makes you unclean. * The sawdust and the plank. * Pharisee and tax collector.	Thomas 45:1 Mark 9:50 Thomas 14:5 Matthew 7:3-5 Luke 18:10-14a
4. Openness	* Sun rises on the good and the bad. * Loving only people who love you. * The barren fig tree. * The dinner party. * The vineyard owner and his tenants.	Matthew 5:45b Matthew 5:46 Luke 13:6-9 Luke 14:16-23 Thomas 65:1-7
4 Care for Others	* Go hungry. * The lost coin. * The good Samaritan. * A generous vineyard owner.	Thomas 69:2 Luke 15:8-10 Luke 10:30-35 Matthew 20:1-15
5 Forgiveness	* Forgive our debts as we have forgiven our debtors. * Forgive and you will be forgiven. * Love your enemies. * Do not resist an evil person. * The king's unjust servant. * Two sons and their father.	Luke 11:2b-4 Luke 6:37 Matthew 5:44 Matthew 5:39-42a Matthew 18:23-33 Luke 15:11-32

Group studies can be very fruitful using this guide. You might start by discussing one or two of the seven opening sections about the nature of the Good Society, then take one of the five qualities that we should possess as members of it. Each week for five weeks, discuss what these ideas mean to you and how they may be explained to other people. Write your own modern parable as a group exercise, remembering that Jesus used parables frequently as the best method of getting people's attention and understanding.

One of the provocative aspects of Jesus' method of teaching was his frequent use of exaggeration, like the camel squeezing through the eye of the needle. Another was the way in which he picked on the bad guy, like the prodigal son and the sly steward, to be the hero of the story! Most importantly, Jesus did not give his listeners all the answers—he left them something to think about. Perhaps you could write a play or movie script for others to watch your story, and leave your audience with some thinking to do when it's over.

Now is our opportunity to take the plain—but demanding—teaching that Jesus left with us and to put it into practice. We can all build a Good Society together. I've given you a few clues; even a child can do it. Will you join in the fun?

APPENDIX I
Notes On The Biblical Text

Where alternative gospel references are given in the notes below, readers will usually find one gospel identified by bold type as the main source, though some amalgamation may have taken place. My translation is based on the Greek text of the four gospels and of the less well-known Gospel of Thomas.

Some scholars view the authenticity of Thomas' sayings, which has a Gnostic bias, with some caution. Their reticence is understandable, but remembering that this gospel probably pre-dated the other four by several years, we may trust its text to deliver some individual phrases attributed to Jesus with more authenticity.

It may be puzzling to Bible students to find that sections of my text are taken from different evangelists. This is one result of the detailed analysis by scholars, discussed earlier. Please refer in the bibliography in Appendix II to the Jesus Seminar's work of textual analysis.

Indications of date include references to "CE" (Common Era = AD), and "BCE" (Before Common Era = BC). These designations are universally employed in multi-religious scholarship.

Abbreviations used in the notes are:
    Mt ~ The Gospel of Matthew
    Mk ~ The Gospel of Mark
    Lk ~ The Gospel of Luke
    Jn ~ The Gospel of John
    Th ~ The Gospel of Thomas

Jesus' Prayer

(1) **Lk 11:2b-4**; see also Mt 6:9-12

The arrangement and brevity of the prayer that Jesus taught his students is quite distinctive. Its hallmark is the use of the Aramaic diminutive "Abba" (Daddy). The use of "Father" was common at the time, but not in Jesus' familiar form. It was typical for teachers to create prayers and sayings for students to learn. The substance of Jesus' prayer was not new, but rather a pithy condensation of existing prayers that was memorized and handed down. The prayer adopts the indirect form of the Hebrew *Kiddush*, and avoids a direct command. "Hallowed" and "holy" are not exact translations. The

Greek is best translated "reverenced," "sanctified," or "made sacred."

The idea of the appearance of the Kingdom was fairly common at that time, and can be found in contemporary rabbinical writings. In the phrase used concerning "daily bread," the original Greek word is very rare, which has led to some uncertainty. Chrysostom and Cyril of Jerusalem preferred the meaning "necessary" (the bread we need), while Coptic sources and Cyril of Alexandria promoted the translation "tomorrow" (our spiritual bread). So the choice is between physical sustenance and long-lasting spiritual nourishment. Jesus may have played deliberately with this ambiguity.

In *The Prayers of Jesus*, Joachim Jeremias quotes a non-canonical saying of Jesus: "No one can obtain the kingdom of Heaven who has not passed through temptation." This saying "testifies to the fact that the concluding petition of the Lord's Prayer does not request that he [*sic*] who prays may be spared temptation, but that God may help him overcome it." Jesus may also have had in mind such sayings as 1 Maccabees 2:49: "My son, when you come to serve the Lord, prepare your soul for temptation."

An earlier rabbinic version of a prayer Jesus may have used as the outline for his own is found in Dr. Israel Abraham's *Studies in Pharisaism and the Gospels*. This prayer reads:

> Our Father in heaven. Hallowed be your exalted name in the world, which you created according to your will. May your kingdom and your lordship come speedily, and be acknowledged by all the world, that your name may be praised in all eternity. May your will be done in heaven and also on earth. Give tranquility of spirit to those who fear you, yet in all things do what seems good to you. Let us enjoy the bread daily apportioned to us. Forgive us, Father, for we have sinned. Forgive also all who have done us injury, even as we forgive all. And lead us not into temptation, but keep us far from all evil. For yours is the greatness and the power and the dominion, the victory and the majesty—yes, in all heaven and on earth. Yours is the kingdom and you are Lord of all beings for ever. Amen.

What is the Kingdom?

(2) **Mk 10:14b**; see also Mt 19:14; Lk 18:16b

Children may be dependent and receptive but are not necessarily humble, though they know they are not fully grown or possessed of full understanding. What is unique about them is their capacity to act at once on what they are taught.

(3) **Mt 13:33**; see also Lk 13:20-21; Th 96:1-2

This saying may refer to a passage in Genesis 18:1-16, where Abraham's wife, Sarah, bakes bread for visiting angels. As in Genesis, the amount of flour used by the woman in the parable is significant. Three *seahs* (measures), estimated to be a bushel of flour, is a very large amount. This, according to Sherman and Johnson, "calls attention to the vastness of the world the kingdom must transform secretly and irresistibly."

(4) **Th 20:2-3**; see also Mt 13:31-32; Mk 4:30-32; Lk 13:18-19

The Jesus Seminar scholars regard this saying from the Gospel of Thomas, and some other of Thomas' verses listed below, as being the closest to the original words of Jesus.

Mustard bushes grow in Israel to a height of about ten feet (3 meters). Mustard was a field plant, not permitted in gardens, and its relatively small size suggests a use of exaggeration by Jesus. It refers to Nebuchadnezzar's dream of a large tree under which cattle sheltered, whose branches provided perches for birds.

The phrase "Birds of Heaven" is a contemporary term for the Gentile nations. This suggests that, just as one rather ordinary herb grows to be all embracing, so the Kingdom will grow astonishingly, from small beginnings, to embrace all people, everywhere.

(5)**Th 107:1-3** with **Mt 18:12-13** and **Lk 15:4-6**

I opted for the brief version of the parable in a form close to Thomas' story. Each evangelist has added a different ending to this saying, so none is shown to have been the original. Thomas' unique use of "The Kingdom of God" as the introduction to the saying ties in with Jesus' other sayings. Thomas gives a quite different message from that of the other gospel writers, however. His opening phrase transforms the story into a parable of the Kingdom. Like the illustrations of bread-making and of the mustard bush, it is the larger passive elements (bread, bush, and flock) that represent the Kingdom, while the active elements (yeast rising, seed growing, and shepherd searching) represent the efforts of those, including Jesus himself, who work actively to bring about the renewal of human society.

When will the Kingdom Come?

(6) **Th 113:2-4**; See also Lk 17:20b-21

This passage suggests that there is nothing spectacular in the arrival of the Kingdom. On the contrary, it is already in existence and is now growing. Hugh J. Schonfield translates Luke's version of this saying: "The Kingdom of God will not come by [your] keeping a sharp look-out for it. Neither is it going to be said, 'Here it is!' or 'There it is!' for the Kingdom of God is right beside you." (*The Original New Testament*)

(7) **Mk 4:26-29**; see also Th 21:9

In *The Parables of the Kingdom*, C. H. Dodd suggests that the story implies that the Kingdom is already present, as seen in God's long dealing with humanity, which is represented in the parable by nature. Alternative views are that the Kingdom is seen in the action of the farmer, or in the seeds' secret growth, or in the miracle of the harvest. The final reference to the farmer's getting out the sickle is probably a reference to the Great Harvest in Joel 3:13, to which all the nations will come at a time of divine judgment.

What will the Kingdom Change?

(8) **Mk 4:3-8**; see also Mt 13:3-8; Lk 8:5-8a; Th 9:1-5

Is the sower of the seed the teacher himself? One view of the parable sees Jesus as the Sower. The seed is the dynamic creative principle or energy at work in society, developing slowly until the whole society is transformed. Dr. Albert Schweitzer saw this as "the movement of repentance awakened by John the Baptist and carried further by the preaching of Jesus" (*Leben Jesu - Forschung*). One gospel view contrasts the various ways in which people hear Jesus' teaching and respond to it.

The explanation given in the main-text commentary, concerning Jesus' dramatic use of exaggerated yields, comes from Joachim Jeremias' insightful assessment of Jesus' actual delivery of the story to his audience (*The Parables of Jesus*). In the agricultural community in which Jesus worked, harvest was the predominant season and thus the inevitable epitome of the successful coming-in of the Kingdom. "Lift up your eyes and look at the fields that they are white for harvest" (Jn 4:35).

(9) **Mt 7:9-11**; see also Lk 11:11-13

Textual confusion over the requests (Mt. bread or fish; Lk. fish or egg) and the unworthy gifts (Mt. stone or snake; Lk. snake or scorpion) in the two gospel records led to a variety of English translations. Funk & Hoover (*The Five Gospels*) suggest that matching Bread with Stone is logical, as the flat pita bread baked in the area is similar in appearance to a round, flat stone. The pairing of Fish with Snake is the most likely original match, as a fish can be like an eel, and may resemble a snake fairly closely. The alternatives, egg and scorpion, defy logical explanation. This is a good example of the choices that scholars grapple with when seeking the original version of a saying.

The Great Consolation

(10) **Lk 6:20b-21**; see also Mt 5:3-4 & 6; Th 54:1

T. W. Manson, in *The Teaching of Jesus*, quotes Psalm 69:32, "The poor will see and be glad—you who seek God, may your hearts live." At the time of Jesus the word "poor" was almost an equivalent for "faithful in religion," while the "rich" were seen as flirting with faiths other than Judaism. There is a contemporary double meaning in each of the phrases. Just as the poor are also seen as the faithful in religion, so the hungry do not only have a physical need but also wait for spiritual nourishment. Those who are crying are not just grieving over their own troubles and losses, but also mourn the sorry state of human society.

(11) **Mt 10:29-31**; see also Lk 12:6-7

The text printed here varies somewhat from that chosen by the Jesus Seminar. It follows a suggestion that the original Aramaic statement did not say the sparrow was "falling to earth," as it is traditionally translated, but merely "landing on the earth." In contrast, Rabbi Simeon ben Jochai (CE 150) wrote: "No bird perishes without God—how much less a man!"

(12) **Mt 6:25-30**; see also Lk 12:22-25 & 27-28; Th 36:1-2

The *Mishnah* puts the same idea beautifully: "Have you ever seen a wild animal or bird practicing a trade? Yet they all have their sustenance without care" (*Kiddushim 4:14*). Old English translations use the metaphor of adding one cubit (the length of a forearm) to one's stature. This meaning is made plain in the light of Psalm 39:5, "Thou hast made my days a mere handbreadth; the span of my years is as nothing before you" (*New International Version*). The old translations spoke of the "lilies of the field" but the original Greek is not specific. The term "wild flowers" is closer to the meaning. Bread was typically baked in ovens fueled by dry grass and flowers—and by dung. (Wood was only available in small amounts in most areas of the country.)

Only Thomas has the opening "from morning to night." Jesus is directing his remarks at those with an overwhelming fixation on their personal needs.

Our Basic Attitudes

(13) **Lk 17:33**; see also Mt 10:39; Mk 8:35; Lk 9:24; Jn 12:25

Scholar George Buttrick once wrote, "A man [*sic*] must forfeit his life as well as his earthly effects in the last day, if he is to share in the glories of the coming age."

(14) **Lk 13:24**; see also Mt 7:13-14

Reference here may be to merchants getting their laden beasts of burden through the gates of a city in the crush immediately preceding the evening curfew. The more heavily loaded the beasts, and thus the wealthier their owners, the harder it was to get the animals in.

(15) **Lk 14:26**; see also Mt 10:37; Th 55:1 & 101:1-3

Many translations use the phrase "if anyone does not <u>hate</u> his father and mother..." The Aramaic original uses a softer word that suggests the idea of "loving something less."

(16) **Lk 9:60b**; see also Mt 8:22b

This saying seems to threaten a drastic break with the established social rules relating to burial. It is clearly one of Jesus' characteristic exaggerations (which may well be why it was remembered). We must go beyond these startling words to see that his demand is to encourage us to cut our ties with the past and embrace the future within the Kingdom.

(17) **Mt 13:44-46**; see also Th 76:1-2 & 109:1-3

Renunciation of wealth is not the point of this saying. Rudolph Otto has written, "The Kingdom is so desirable that out of sheer joy a man [*sic*] will sell all his worldly possessions to have it, and count it no sacrifice whatever" (*The Kingdom of God and The Son of Man*). Some have a problem with Jesus' appearing to condone the hiding of the treasure found in the field, missing his point. This illustration, typical of his teaching, uses the lack of ethics by the treasure finders to heighten the sense of their commitment to the search.

Thomas tells a very different story of the treasure hidden in a field. It is similar in form to a contemporary rabbinic parable. Thomas makes the owner unaware of the treasure, as is his son, who inherits it and then disposes of it. The buyer, however, on plowing the field turns up the treasure. This version may contain Jesus' original meaning, that it is by our own activity that we will discover the Kingdom.

There is an ancient rabbinic parable rather similar to Jesus' story of the pearl of great price. Though they were quite rare, pearls were traded in the Mediterranean region in those days.

(18) **Mk 4:21b**; see also Mt 5:14-15; Lk 8:16, 11:33; Th 33:2-3

The illustration of the light put on the stand is repeated five times in the gospels, each time slightly differently. This demonstrates the Jesus Seminar's rule of evidence, that "Jesus' followers remembered only the gist of his sayings rather than his precise words." Against that, Ludwig Koehler (*Hebrew Man*) showed clearly that small Hebrew communities traditionally memorized sayings, sitting together around the fireside. Some of Jesus' sayings may have been better memorized than others; he may even have varied the content himself from time to time.

The older English translations have the light coming from a candle placed in a candlestick. This is incorrect. Candles were not in use in that area at the time of Jesus.

Giving Up Power And Wealth

(19) **Mt 19:23b-24**; see also Mk 10:23b-25; Lk 18:24b-25

Some scholars have suggested the Greek word translated here as "camel" is incorrect. One fifth-century theory was that the Greek *kamelos* (camel) was incorrectly copied from one manuscript to another and should have read *kamilos*, which is Greek for a rope, or a hawser attached to a ship's anchor. Another old theory is that the word refers to camelhair. Both make it easier for the wealthy to enter the Kingdom. Supporting "camel," however, is a similar saying in the *Qur'an*, and the use of an elephant in a similar context by the *Talmud*.

A theory on the other side of the discussion suggests that the Greek for "eye of a needle" had a subsidiary meaning: "a narrow gorge or gate." The real point in this debate is whether we want to interpret Jesus as saying it is *impossible* for the wealthy to enter the Kingdom, or only that it is *difficult* for them to do so.

What Jesus is saying refutes the contemporary concept that a person's wealth represented a gift or blessing by God, and so it was something they were entitled to own. Difficult or impossible, Jesus asserts unequivocally that wealth is a real spiritual hindrance to participation in the Kingdom. The more we try to wriggle out of the implication of his words, the more we show up our weakness.

(20) **Th 95:1-2; Mt 5:42b; Lk 6:30b, 34a, 35a**

This passage in Thomas has no direct parallels in the canonical gospels. Nevertheless, Matthew and Luke contain similar ideas, leading to the conclusion that this probably was something Jesus said. Of course, if everyone put his words into practice immediately there would be financial chaos. But Jesus is examining our attitude toward others, rather than giving us a blueprint for the exact steps we should be taking.

(21) **Mt 6:3**; see also Th 62:2

T. H. Manson interprets this phrase: "Do not let your closest friend know about your charitable gifts" (*The Sayings of Jesus*).

(22) **Mt 6:24**; see also Lk 16:13; Th 47:2

Material possessions of any kind are *Mammon* in Aramaic, which is the word used in the gospels. The Jewish law permitted a slave to be owned by two masters at that time.

(23) **Th 63:1-3**; see also Lk 12:16b-20

Drawing on older sayings, Jesus points out that the possession of wealth is "no protection against the uncertainty of life" (S. MacLean Gilmour). Since, at our death, our wealth is passed to others, Jesus implies that much greater satisfaction may be found by sharing wealth during our lifetime.

(24) **Mk 12:17; Mt 22:21c; Lk 20:25; Th 100:2b-3**

The tax paid to the Roman authorities was roughly the equivalent of two days' wages at that time.

Shrewdness

(25) **Mt 10:16b**; see also Th 39:3

This passage bridges a gap in Jesus' teaching by way of a paradox. He appears to have wanted his followers to remain connected with the serious problems of living, despite their enthusiasm for the Kingdom. But idealism and pragmatism belong together. We cannot retreat from life.

(26) **Lk 12:58-59**; see also Mt 5:25-26

The word translated *Judge* or *Magistrate* is a Greek term generally used to describe a senior collector of taxes. This illustration may be about a dispute with a minor tax collector being brought for settlement before a district tax court, hence the threat of time in jail.

(27) **Mt 25:14-28; Lk 19:13, 15-24**

Departing from the Jesus Seminar's decision concerning how much money was entrusted and to how many slaves, I have followed Joachim Jeremias' argument, in *The Parables of Jesus*, that the exaggerated sums in Matthew are likely an embellishment, while the smaller sums in Luke are possibly more original. For some reason, Matthew gives the top figure as a huge five talents (75 years' wages for a laborer) to the first servant, then two talents to the second and finally one talent to the third. Luke gives an equal amount of ten minas (30 months' wages for a laborer) to each of ten servants. Not to be caught between two evangelists, I have chosen the smaller number of servants and the smaller sum entrusted to each. Given the significant differences between the gospel records, we should acknowledge that the details of the story were probably the evangelists' best guess. The real importance of the parable, however, is its central issue concerning the servants' unequal acceptance of their responsibilities. This remains Jesus' main point, whatever the details may prove to have been.

Bernard Brandon Scott, in *Hear Then the Parable*, sees the story driving home "the stringent demand on faith to produce an increase or face a tragic judgment."

(28) **Lk 16:1-8a**

T. H. Manson, in *The Sayings of Jesus*, gives the figures as 100 baths of oil (about 86,800 gallons) and 1,083 bushels of wheat.

In *The Parables of the Kingdom*, C. H. Dodd raised the possibility that this parable is a story exposing "the Sadducean priesthood, who made a merit of keeping in with the Romans by concessions which they had no right to make."

It seems unlikely that the landowner would commend a fundamentally dishonest deed. One attractive interpretation, suggested by Howard Marshall

(*New Bible Commentary*), is that the manager might have been involved in collecting bad debts from those who were unable to meet the very high interest charges current at the time. If so, he would be prudent in collecting part of each debt, rather than allowing it to become uncollectable.

John Dominic Crossan (*Servant Parables of Jesus*) and J. D. Derrett (*Fresh Light on the Unjust Steward*) suggest that in cutting the debt owed, the steward failed to gain a sufficient profit for his master, but he also eliminated his own customary profit margin, thereby winning friends among the debtors involved. Thus he earned both praise for his sagacity and a rebuke for being untrustworthy.

Persistent Patience

(29) **Mt 7:7-8**; see also Lk 11:9-10; Th 2:1-2, 92:1 & 94:1-2

The second half of this saying is omitted: "Be quite certain: everyone who asks, receives; seeks, finds; and to those who knock it will be opened." This appears to be a stylistic repetition, adding little to the first half. It seems likely that the original "Ask-Seek-Knock" was a sound-bite Jesus either originated or made his own. (James 4:3 and I Jn 3:22 repeat the phrase in various forms.)

(30) **Lk 18:2-5**

The judge in the story became paranoid that his reputation might be compromised. The literal translation of his words might be, "Lest she come at last and beat me."

(31) **Lk 11:5-8**

The Greek original is confusing and is variously translated. The classical Greek scholar E. V. Rieu (*The Four Gospels*) makes the person in need out to be the speaker; others make him a friend of the speaker. The teacher's point is the same: persistence does the trick.

Honesty And Integrity

(32) **Th 45:1**; see also Mt 7:16b; Lk 6:44b

This saying illustrates the setting of much of Jesus' teaching in the agricultural community of Galilee. He used many illustrations from nature to capture his audience's imagination. The thorn bush symbolizes destruction, while the grapes are symbolic of the enjoyment of life.

(33) **Mk 9:50**; see also Mt 5:13b; Lk 14:34

The gospel writers have each fitted this saying into a context of their own. Salt was a valuable commodity—Roman soldiers were paid in salt—as well as being an important ingredient in cooking. Thus the follower of Jesus (the salt) must maintain integrity and enthusiasm (saltiness).

(34) **Th 14:5**; see also Mt 15:11; Mk 7:15

This may refer to contemporary taboos concerning food (see Acts 10:15). Above all, it is a call for people to control their speaking, and to monitor their thinking before putting their ideas into words.

(35) **Mt 7:3-5**: see also Lk 6:41-42; Th 26:1-2

The Revised Standard Version of the Bible uses "Log" instead of "Plank." Both are correct. The Greek word refers to timber used in building. This saying is a fine example of Jesus' memorable use of exaggeration.

(36) **Lk 18:10-14a**

The Jewish historian Josephus describes the Pharisees as "a body of Jews with a reputation of excelling the rest of their nation in the observances of religion and as exact exponents of the laws." The Pharisee in the story was truly zealous in his observance. He fasted twice a week, although the religious law only required fasting on the Day of Atonement; and he paid tithes on all his income—the law demanded much less. While it seems possible that the original story may have illustrated the hypocrisy of those religious enthusiasts, its main point was the broader one of personal integrity.

Tax collectors were hated members of society, opportunists employed by the occupying Romans to levy tolls and tariffs on their own people. Jesus uses the sharp differences between the most loyal and the least loyal members of the Jewish community to illustrate his point. The tax collector's words start with the opening of Psalm 51, a shorthand allusion to that great prayer of entreaty.

Openness

(37) **Mt 5:45b**

The way in which God permits good and bad people to grow up together becomes for us the foundation upon which our openness, forgiveness, and love toward others can be built. "This is God's way and we are God's children. [Jesus is] not talking about justice, or about helping bad people become good; he's only talking about our being like God" (Carroll Simcox, *The First Gospel*).

(38) **Mt 5:46**; see also Lk 6:32

The word *sinners* was a contemporary term denoting those who either did not know the Law of Moses or who, knowingly, did not keep it.

(39) **Lk 13:6-9**

The fig tree is used as a symbol for Israel in Joel 1:7, Hosea 9:10, and elsewhere. Jesus sees that his own people should be the first to embrace the Kingdom and *bear fruit* as the parable suggests. Leviticus 19:23 required that all new trees be allowed three years' growth before harvesting. The implication is that the tree (Israel) is still young and deserves more time to fulfill God's intentions. Compare John the Baptist: "Any tree that fails to produce good fruit will be cut down and thrown into the fire" (Mt 3:10).

(40) **Lk 14:16-23; Th 64:1-12**; see also Mt 22:1-14

Because of many variations in the gospels, this story is told here in its shortest form. How much of this story was Jesus' own? There was a Jewish tale, dating from at least 500 BCE, which told of a tax collector seeking to ingratiate himself with local society leaders by inviting them to dinner. He also was rebuffed. So that the food might not be wasted he invited the poor instead.

In the Torah, Deuteronomy 24:5 laid down that a newly married man was free from military service and from all other duties for one year—an insightful piece of social legislation.

(41) **Th 65:1-7**; see also Mt 21:33-39; Mk 12:1-8; Lk 20:9-15a

Thomas' gospel is chosen for its freedom from editorial additions. Payment-in-kind of rent due was usual at the time.

Care For Others

(42) **Th 69:2**

There are no exact parallels in the synoptic gospels, although the Beatitudes (Mt 5:6 and Lk 6:21) come close. Burton L. Mack *(The Lost Gospel)* notes that the gospel source Q says, "How fortunate the hungry—they will be fed." So it may be that Thomas has recorded this saying turned inside out in a way that is quite typical of Jesus' method of creating memorable phrases.

(43) **Lk 15:8-10**

The piece of silver was probably a drachma, worth about two or three days' wages, part of the woman's dowry and an essential domestic reserve against poverty.

(44) **Lk 10:30-35**

The 17-mile (27 km.) road from Jerusalem to Jericho descends 3,300 ft. (1,000 m.) into the valley. Jericho was a town where priests relaxed after service in the Temple at Jerusalem. There was a steady traffic of the religious between the cities. Eta Linnemann *(Parables of Jesus)* suggests it would not have surprised people at the time that the story painted the Priest and Levite as unmerciful, because the priesthood was in bad repute. But choosing a Samaritan as the hero was truly surprising.

There was a mixed population in Samaria of Israelites, taken captive by the Assyrians in 722 BCE, and the heathen people with whom they had intermarried. The religion of Israel was not strictly observed there, and contact with them by the majority of Jews was avoided. Thus the only thing the Samaritan had in common with Jesus' audience was his humanity.

The oil and wine used by the Samaritan were commonly used as curative agents at that time.

(45) **Mt 20:1-15**

There was a rabbinic parable, told at the funeral of Rabbi Bun bar Hijja in 325 BCE, with close similarity to Jesus' story, except for a very different ending. It appears Jesus adapted this tale. R. T. France comments, "No one was underpaid; it was just that some [workers] were treated with unreasonable generosity."

Leviticus 19:13 and Deuteronomy 24:15 require payment of wages at the end of the day. But pay for how much work? "If they go home with wages for only a single hour, their families cannot be fed" (Joachim Jeremias, *Die Gleichnisse Jesu*). Their need for a whole day's wage was recognized and generously met. The metaphor in this parable for the "unreasonable" mercy and loving-kindness of God is inescapable.

Forgiveness

(46) **Lk 6:37c**; see also Mt 6:14-15; Mk 11:25

This is an early saying which has its roots in the wisdom literature of the Old Testament (Proverbs 11:17). Forgiveness is an essential part of the prayer of Jesus, both for people seeking to live in harmony, and for individuals in relationship with God.

(47) **Mt 5:44**; see also Lk 6:27

The root meaning of the word we translate "Love" is generally misunderstood. It is a practical emotion, lacking sentimentality, leading toward harmonious living. This phrase is an extension of earlier teaching in Leviticus 19:18 and Proverbs 25:21-22.

(48) **Mt 5:39-42a**; see also Lk 6:29-30a

The Greek text may mean either "an evil person" or "an evil thing." Jesus does not say that we should give way to evil by refusing to stand up against it, but that we should not take physical force as the means of our resistance or revenge.

The coat of the common man at that time was a sleeved tunic, and his overcoat a cloak that was used as a blanket at night.

The conscription referred to was begun by the royal Persian mail, whose couriers could lawfully press people into limited service. It was continued by later occupying powers in that area, including the Roman army.

(49) **Mt 18:23-33**

Several commentators suggest the debtor was an official in the service of the king, not a personal servant. This explains the possibility of an immense debt. R. T. France comments that in the Greek text the sum of 10,000 talents combines the largest Greek numeral with the most valuable unit of currency, so it was the largest sum imaginable. In comparison, the fellow servant's debt was a tiny fraction of that amount. This gross imbalance made it ludicrous for the official not to forgive his fellow.

Scholars are uncertain whether the king in the story was meant to symbolize God. But this story vividly illustrates Jesus' prayer, "Forgive us our debts as we have forgiven our debtors." Divine forgiveness is not unconditional; if the official was not prepared to be forgiving of the minor debt, he was already in slavery to his possessions, so his subsequent imprisonment has been seen as an appropriate metaphor.

The gospel ends, "The king was so angry he had him imprisoned until he paid back all he owed"(v.34), adding an explanation of the story for its readers (v.35). Contrary to the inclusion of v.34 by the Jesus Seminar, I have followed H. C. Kee's suggestion (*Interpreter's Bible*) that "it is quite likely the original parable ended with the king's question, which drives home the point about forgiveness," concluding that the man's imprisonment was an editorial addition which should be omitted.

(50) **Lk 15:11-32**

The story is not primarily about the "Prodigal Son" but about both young men and their relationship with their father and with each other.

In Jewish law, owners had the right to dispose of property either by will or lifetime gift, which was rarely made. Here, the younger son took possession of his share; the father retained a life-interest in the elder brother's estate. However the inheritance issue is not central to the story.

The parable may have sprung out of a popular saying: "When the Children of Israel are reduced to eating carob pods, they will repent." The Talmud also has a saying: "When a son has to walk barefoot, he remembers how well he was treated in his father's house." Jesus used his sources well.

Appendix II
A Brief Bibliography

Here are some paperbacks about modern New Testament scholarship and basic books on other faiths. Included also are books mentioned in the text, President Jefferson's synopsis of Jesus' teaching, and Naomi Drew's educational primer on peaceful relationships.

The Jefferson Bible: The Life and Morals of Jesus Thomas Jefferson. Essays by F. Forrester Church and Jaroslav Pelikan. Beacon Press™ 1989
The Five Gospels: The Search for the Authentic Words of Jesus Robert Funk, Roy W Hoover, and The Jesus Seminar. HarperSanFrancisco™ 1997
The Lost Gospel: The Book of Q and Christian Origins Burton L. Mack. HarperSanFrancisco™ 1994
Who Wrote The New Testament Burton L. Mack. Harper Collins™ 1995
The Gospel Of Thomas Marvin Meyer. HarperSanFrancisco™ 1992
Hear Then The Parable: A Commentary on the Parables Bernard Brandon Scott. Fortune Press™ 1989
The Once And Future Jesus Marcus Borg, John Dominic Crossan, et al. Polebridge Press™ 1999
Once And Future Faith Karen Armstrong, Don Cupitt. Polebridge Press™ 2001
Honest To Jesus Robert W. Funk. Polebridge Press™ 1996
Learning The Skills Of Peacemaking Naomi Drew. Jalmar Press™ 1999
Hinduism For Today Carrie Mercier. Oxford University Press 1998
Islam For Today Angela Wood. Oxford University Press 1998
Judaism For Today Angela Wood. Oxford University Press 1997
The Heart Of The Buddha's Teaching Tich Nhat Hanh. Broadway 1999
The World's Religions Huston Smith. HarperSanFrancisco™ 1991

www.ingramcontent.com/pod-product-compliance
Lightning Source LLC
Chambersburg PA
CBHW071441160426
43195CB00013B/1991